Better Homes and Gardens®
CHRISTMAS
FROM THE HEART®

Volume 14

Meredith® Books
Des Moines, Iowa

Better Homes and Gardens®

CHRISTMAS
FROM THE HEART®

Editor:	Carol Field Dahlstrom
Writers:	Susan M. Banker, Winifred Moranville
Assistant Art Director:	Todd Emerson Hanson
Copy Chief:	Terri Fredrickson
Publishing Operations Manager:	Karen Schirm
Edit and Design Production Coordinator:	Mary Lee Gavin
Editorial Assistant:	Cheryl Eckert, Kairee Windsor
Marketing Product Managers:	Aparna Pande, Isaac Petersen, Gina Rickert, Stephen Rogers, Brent Wiersma, Tyler Woods
Book Production Managers:	Pam Kvitne, Marjorie J. Schenkelberg, Rick von Holdt, Mark Weaver
Contributing Copy Editor:	Judy Friedman
Contributing Proofreaders	Genelle Deist, Karen Grossman, Sara Henderson
Cover Photographer:	Pete Krumhardt
Photographers:	Andy Lyons Cameraworks, Pete Krumhardt, Scott Little, Jay Wilde
Technical Illustrator:	Chris Neubauer Graphics, Inc.
Project Designers:	Susan M. Banker, Heidi Boyd, Carol Dahlstrom, Kristin Detrick, Margaret Sindelar, Ann E. Smith
Photostyling Assistant:	Kristin Detrick

MEREDITH® BOOKS

Executive Director, Editorial:	Gregory H. Kayko
Executive Director, Design:	Matt Strelecki
Senior Editor/Group Manager:	Jan Miller
Senior Associate Design Director:	Ken Carlson
Publisher and Editor in Chief:	James D. Blume
Editorial Director:	Linda Raglan Cunningham
Executive Director, Marketing:	Jeffrey B. Myers
Executive Director, New Business Development:	Todd M. Davis
Executive Director, Sales:	Ken Zagor
Director, Operations:	George A. Susral
Director, Production:	Douglas M. Johnston
Business Director:	Jim Leonard

Vice President and General Manager:	Douglas J. Guendel

BETTER HOMES AND GARDENS® MAGAZINE
Editor in Chief:	Karol DeWulf Nickell

MEREDITH PUBLISHING GROUP
President:	Jack Griffin
Senior Vice President:	Bob Mate

MEREDITH CORPORATION
Chairman and Chief Executive Officer:	William T. Kerr
President and Chief Operating Officer:	Stephen M. Lacy
In Memoriam:	E.T. Meredith III (1933-2003)

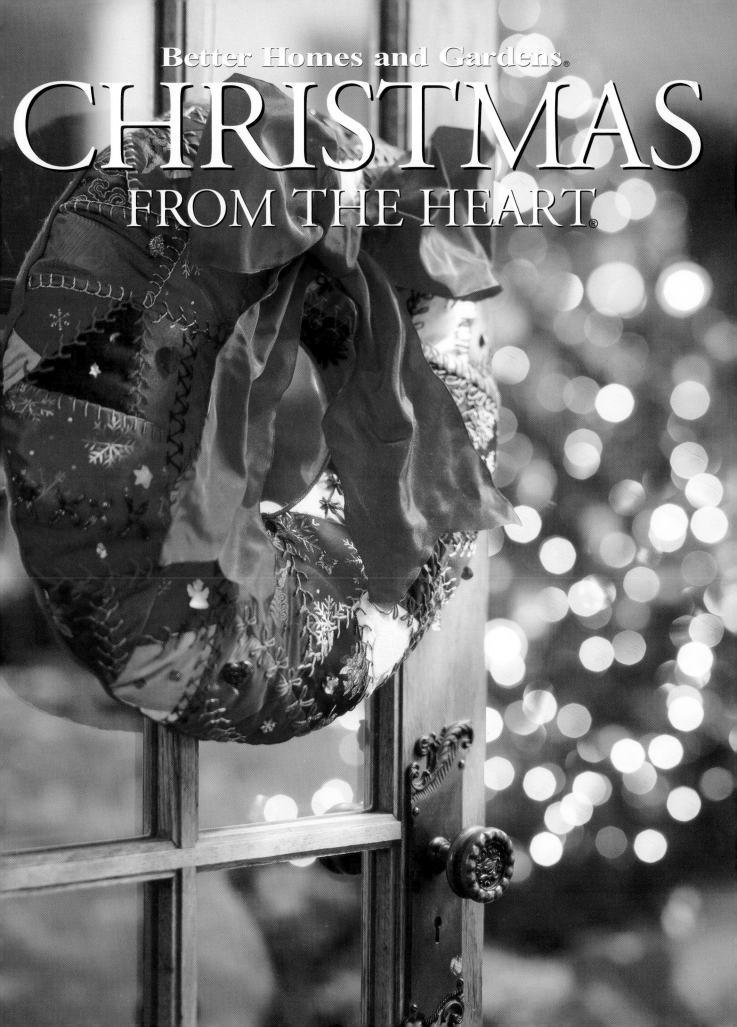

Better Homes and Gardens®
CHRISTMAS
FROM THE HEART®

contents

pretty & pastel

Create a lovely holiday atmosphere with unexpected soft colors gracing everything from your tree to your tabletop.

Hanging from a white-as-snow tree, these pastel Christmas confections are crafted from clay for years of enjoyment. The **So-Sweet Cupcakes** are frosted with color and nestled into silver cups. With tiny bead sprinkles, the **Snowflake Cookies** look just as delicious as fresh treats from the oven. Instructions are on *page 16.*

7

These trims are so much fun to make, you'll want to create them by the dozen! Frosted and covered with colorful sprinkles, **Delightful Doughnuts** are especially sweet on a holiday tree. The **Hot Cocoa Cups** look as though they're hot, but these clever trims are oh-so-cool! To light up your home for the season, blanket a votive holder with a pretty pastel ornament design to make a **Very Merry Votive Candleholder,** *opposite*. Instructions are on *pages 16–17*.

Your tabletop and mantel will shine with festive decorations in all your favorite pastel hues. Cobalt, purple, and teal combine with soft lavender as an unexpected, glorious surprise on a star-topped **Merry Mosaic Tree.** When time is short, **Banded Pillars** make for a striking centerpiece. Pretty pink and green satin fabrics are embellished with dainty machine and hand stitches on a **Festive Floral Stocking,** *opposite*. Instructions and pattern are on *pages 18–21.*

Glass and glitter on this pair of projects reflect Christmas lights with a beautiful glow. Transformed from plain glass containers and simple candles to **Beaded Beauties**, these dazzling table accessories are easy to make for happy housewarmings. Artificial **Snow-Laden Pears,** *opposite*, are painted, stenciled, and dusted with glitter to display all winter long. Instructions are on *page 21*.

Choose your favorite pastel colors to make romantic ornaments and cute contemporary stockings. Once flea market finds, Victorian **Silverware Ornaments,** *opposite*, become elegant trims with dainty porcelain flowers and sheer ribbon bows. Choose soft polar fleece for a **Jolly Jester Stocking** to hold special surprises from Santa. Instructions and pattern are on *pages 22–23.*

So-Sweet Cupcakes

shown on pages 6–8

WHAT YOU NEED

Air-dry clay, such as Crayola
   Model Magic, in white, yellow,
   green, red, and blue
Foil candy cups; eye pin
Pastel-color pearl beads
1/8-inch-wide satin ribbon
1/2-inch-wide sheer ribbon

HERE'S HOW

1 Blend two parts white clay with one part yellow clay to make the cupcake batter. Roll a small handful of batter into a smooth ball and place it in a foil candy cup. Gently squeeze the foil cup so that the pleats are embedded in the clay and the top of the cupcake is extending over the top edge of the cup.

2 To blend frosting, add a small pinch of red clay to white clay to make pink, or add a small pinch of green clay to white clay to make mint green. Roll the mixed frosting into a small ball (the size of a quarter) and press it flat. Lay it on the cupcake, adding a second frosting layer if desired. Press pearl bead sprinkles into the top layer. Insert an eye pin into the center of the cupcake. Let it dry.

3 Tie a small length of satin ribbon in a decorative bow just below the opening in the eye pin. Thread sheer ribbon through the eye pin to make a hanging loop. Bring the ends together and tie them in a knot.

Delightful Doughnuts

shown on pages 6–8

WHAT YOU NEED

Air-dry clay, such as Crayola Model
   Magic, in white, yellow, green,
   blue, and red
1½-inch wood wheel; toothpick
Tiny pearl beads
1/8-inch-wide sheer ribbons

HERE'S HOW

1 Mix two parts white clay to one part yellow clay to make the light yellow doughnut dough. Cover the wood wheel with a 1/4-inch-thick layer of dough.

2 Roll the doughnut to smooth the outside edges. Insert and rotate a toothpick into the center of the covered donut to clear out the center hole.

3 To make the frosting, roll a 1/4-inch-thick coil of white clay and pinch it flat. Lay the uneven flattened frosting around one side of the doughnut.

4 To make sprinkles, roll tiny coils of clay and cut them into 1/4-inch-long pieces; press directly into the white frosting. Press pearl beads into the clay. Let the clay dry.

5 Thread a hanging string through the center hole of the doughnut and bring the ends together. Tie them in an overhand knot.

6 Tie a ribbon into a decorative bow on the hanging thread next to the doughnut center.

Snowflake Cookies

shown on pages 6–7

WHAT YOU NEED

Rolling pin or pasta machine
   designated for clay use only
Polymer clay in tan and white
Snowflake cookie cutter
Glass seed and bugle beads in
   white, blue, and pink
Toothpick
Silver embroidery floss

HERE'S HOW

1 Work the tan clay until it's smooth and pliable. Roll it to a 1/4-inch-thick sheet using a rolling pin or pasta machine.

2 Press the cookie cutter down into the clay and lift out a cut cookie.

3 Knead the white clay frosting and smooth it to a 1/8-inch-thick sheet. Press the cookie cutter into the white clay and lift out the snowflake-shape frosting. Pinch each snowflake end off the frosting. Smooth under the torn ends and then place the prepared frosting over the tan cookie.

4 Sprinkle the glass beads over the frosting and press each bead down into the clay so the bead holes are concealed. Use a toothpick to pierce a single hanging hole 1/8 inch down from the top of one snowflake point. Bake the finished cookie according to the clay manufacturer's directions.

5 Thread an embroidery floss hanging string through the hole in the top of the cookie. Bring the floss ends together and tie them in an overhand knot.

Very Merry Votive Candleholder

shown on page 9

WHAT YOU NEED

Transparent ornament-shape
   sticker to fit one side of
   candleholder
Glass votive candleholder
Paintbrush; decoupage medium,
   such as Mod Podge
Gold micro mini beads
Votive candle

HERE'S HOW

1 Center the sticker on the front of the votive candleholder. Press the sticker onto the surface of the glass.
2 Brush the sticker with decoupage medium. While the decoupage medium is wet, sprinkle it with gold micro mini beads. Let it dry.
3 Place votive candle in the holder.

Note: *Never leave burning candles unattended.*

WHAT YOU NEED

White air-dry clay, such as Crayola
   Model Magic
Brown air-dry clay (or combine
   pinches of red, blue, yellow,
   and green)
White china espresso cup
¼-inch-wide satin ribbon
¼-inch-wide sheer ribbon

HERE'S HOW

1 Roll three pieces of white clay to resemble miniature marshmallows for each mug ornament. Let them dry while you prepare the hot chocolate.
2 Combine a grape-size ball of brown clay with a small handful of white clay. Knead the two together until the white is almost completely incorporated into the brown and it looks like hot chocolate. If it's too dark, add more white clay, or if it's too light, add more brown. Once pleased with the color, place the light brown hot chocolate into the cup. Pinch and swirl the top surface of the clay for added interest.
3 Set marshmallows into the dips in the clay surface. Let the clay air dry.
4 Tie a satin ribbon bow on the cup handle. Tie a sheer hanging ribbon to the handle.

Merry Mosaic Tree

shown on page 10

WHAT YOU NEED

Tracing paper; pencil
Lightweight embossing brass
  sheet, such as Art Emboss
Embossing tool or ballpoint pen
Scissors
4×9-inch plastic-foam cone
Crafts knife
Clear silicone sealer adhesive
Newspapers
4-foot length of brass ball chain
Straight pins
Acrylic mosaic pieces, such as
  Clearly Mosaics, in cobalt,
  purple, and teal
Small piece of clay (optional)
Eggplant acrylic paint
Plastic bowl; crafts stick
Ivory grout
Disposable or rubber gloves
Sponge

HERE'S HOW

1 Trace star pattern, *right*, onto tracing paper. Trace the pattern onto brass sheet using an embossing tool or ballpoint pen; emboss dots at edge. Cut out the brass star. Draw free-form triangles on brass sheet; embellish with dots. Cut out the triangles.

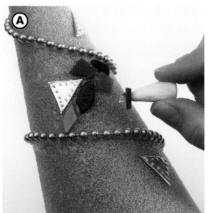

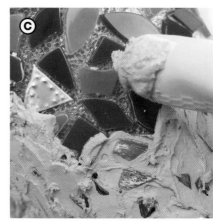

2 Make a slit in the top of the cone and using a crafts knife insert brass star. Glue star in place using silicone sealer.

3 Spread out newspapers on a work surface. Adhere the ball chain to the cone starting at the top. Apply a thin line of sealer to the cone and press the ball chain in place. Use straight pins to hold the ball chain in place while the silicone dries. Apply sealer to the back of the brass triangles and adhere randomly on the cone.

4 Pick up mosaic pieces using a small piece of clay. Apply sealer to the back of each mosaic piece and press it onto the cone. Place the mosaic pieces randomly on the cone, leaving small gaps between pieces as shown in Photo A, *opposite*. Let the sealer dry 24 hours.

5 Follow the manufacturer's directions to grout the acrylic pieces. To color the grout, mix water and acrylic paint in a bowl with a crafts stick, as shown in Photo B, *opposite*. Gradually add powder grout to form a putty consistency. Put on gloves. Press grout into spaces between mosaic pieces, as shown in Photo C, *opposite*. Wait 10 minutes; remove excess grout with a damp sponge. Let grout dry 24 hours before using the tree.

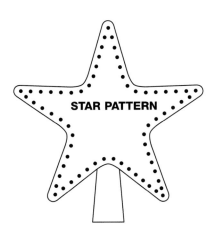

STAR PATTERN

**Merry Mosaic Tree
Full-Size Star Pattern**

Banded Pillars

shown on page 10

WHAT YOU NEED

Purple pillar candles
Rubbing alcohol
Paper towels; rubber bands
Ruler
Acrylic paints in purple, eggplant, royal fuchsia, and metallic silver
Candle- and soap-painting medium, such as Delta Ceramcoat
Paintbrush
Crafts knife; side cutters
Silver-head straight pins
Thin molding strips, such as Making Memories variety bead, spindle, and bead (available in scrapbooking stores)
Scissors
Silver mini brads

HERE'S HOW

1 Wipe the surface of the pillar candles with paper towels moistened with rubbing alcohol. Put rubber bands on pillars to designate areas of candles that will be painted. Use a ruler to line up the rubber bands evenly.

2 Mix the acrylic paint with an equal amount of candle and soap painting medium. Paint each candle a different color using a brush; let dry. Mix equal parts of metallic silver paint and candle- and soap-painting medium. Lightly brush on pillars using different directions of paint strokes on each candle. Let dry. Before removing rubber bands from candles, score painted edges touching the rubber bands with a crafts knife to keep paint from pulling away from candle.

3 Using side cutters, snip off approximately ½ inch of the sharp ends of several straight pins. Starting with one pillar, bend a molding strip around the pillar. Cut off the excess, leaving a very slight gap where molding ends meet to allow a mini brad to pass through. Peel off the adhesive strip backing and press the molding onto candle. Insert a brad into the center of the gap where the molding meets. Insert two shortened straight pins in the gap above and below the brad. Press securely into the candle. Repeat this procedure to adhere the remaining molding strips.

Note: *Never leave burning candles unattended.*

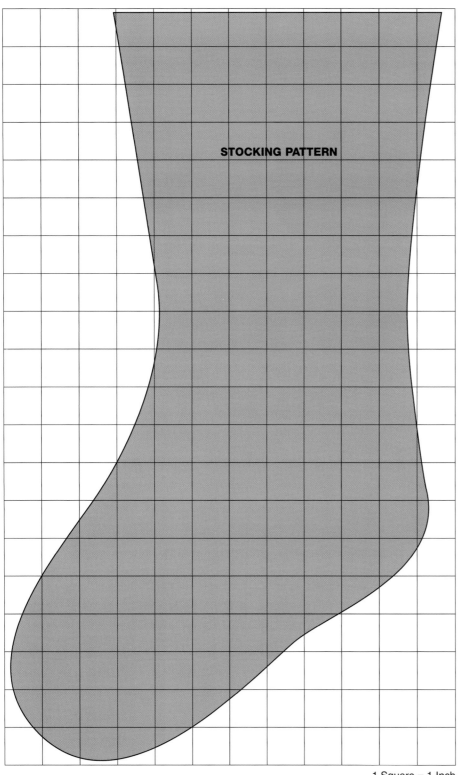

STOCKING PATTERN

Festive Floral Stocking Pattern
Enlarge 250%

1 Square = 1 Inch

Festive Floral Stocking

shown on page 11

WHAT YOU NEED

⅝ yard of pink decorator fabric for
   front and back

Scissors

Tape measure

Batting

Metallic gold machine thread

Sewing machine

Pencil

Tracing paper

Straight pins

1¾ yards of gold sew-in piping

⅝ yard of green satin fabric for
   lining and ruffle

Sewing needle

Ribbon floss in green and pink

Beads in 4 mm and 6 mm sizes in
   iridescent, pink, and green

3 yards of ⅝-inch pink picot-edge
   ribbon

HERE'S HOW

1 For stocking front, cut a 16×24-inch piece of decorator fabric. Line the cut fabric with batting; machine-quilt as desired using gold metallic thread.

2 Enlarge and trace the stocking pattern, *opposite*. Cut out the pattern. Pin the shape on the quilted piece and baste around the shape. Remove pattern. Stitch sew-in piping along stocking shape except at top edge. Cut out the stocking front, allowing ½-inch seam allowance. Use the pattern to cut backing fabric from pink and two lining pieces from green satin.

3 Detail the stocking front working ribbon floss in straight stitches, lazy daisies, and French knots, as illustrated *below* and on *page 35*. Add beads at random in groups

Straight Stitch

of three. Stitch stocking front to back, right sides facing, leaving toe edge open for turning. Repeat with lining pieces, leaving an opening for turning. Trim and clip seam allowance; turn stocking to right side.

4 For ruffle cut a 36-inch-long strip of green satin fabric 3½ inches wide. Seam short ends together. Press ruffle in half lengthwise, wrong sides facing. Gather ruffle to fit top edge of stocking. Stitch ruffle around top edge of stocking. Add ribbon for fabric loop at back seam.

5 Keeping ruffle free from seam, slip stocking into lining, right sides facing, matching seams. Stitch around top edge. Pull stocking though lining opening. Stitch the opening closed. Smooth lining into stocking with ruffle pointed upward. Topstitch around top edge of stocking through all layers.

6 Cut three 18-inch-long pieces of ribbon. Tie ribbons into a bow. Stitch the ribbon in place.

Beaded Beauties

shown on page 12

WHAT YOU NEED

Double-sided tape in various widths
Glass candleholders
Scissors
Very fine beads
Thick candles
Fine wire
Beads for stringing on wire
Wire cutter

HERE'S HOW

1 Apply double-sided tape to the candleholders where bead designs are desired. To make triangles, use wide tape and cut into shapes. Peel off the protective backing from the tape.

2 Sprinkle beads onto sticky tape until covered well.

3 Decorate the candles in the same manner as the candleholders, being careful to use only very thick candles so the lit wick will not come in contact with the tape and beads.

4 To add beaded wire, cut wire the desired length. String beads onto wire and form into any shape. Tie or wrap the wire around the candles.

Note: *Never leave burning candles unattended.*

Snow-Laden Pears

shown on pages 12–13

WHAT YOU NEED

Rag
Artificial pale yellow pears
Rubbing alcohol
Paintbrush and water
Acrylic pearl paints in pink, green, yellow, and white
Snowflake stencil
Palette knife
Texturizing opaque white gel
White glitter

HERE'S HOW

1 Wipe off surface of pears with a cloth dampened with rubbing alcohol.

2 Paint surface of pears in blended colors. Brush a thin coat of paint onto pear. Blend colors like pink and yellow or green and yellow, adding white where softer colors are desired. Let dry.

3 Paint on more coats if desired. Applying only two coats leaves a transparent look. Let dry.

4 Hold a snowflake stencil on the pear. Using a palette knife, apply a small amount of gel over the shape, spreading it on thick enough to create a dimensional snowflake design.

5 Sprinkle glitter onto the wet gel. Let dry, turn, and repeat on other side.

6 Arrange the pears in a bowl or hang as ornaments.

Silverware Ornaments

shown on page 14

WHAT YOU NEED
Wire cutters
Artificial flowers, such as porcelain
  (available in the wedding crafts
  section of a crafts store)
Hot-glue gun and glue sticks
Silverware
Wired ribbon and scissors
Thin wire or nylon string

HERE'S HOW
1 Trim artificial flower stems to fit onto the silverware.
2 Use dots of hot glue to attach flowers to silverware.
3 Tie a generous sheer ribbon bow on the handle.
4 Use thin wire or nylon string to tie a loop around the handle for hanging.

Jolly Jester Stocking

shown on page 15

WHAT YOU NEED
Tracing paper
Pencil
Scissors
½ yard pastel polar fleece
¼ yard white polar fleece
Matching thread
Sewing machine
18-inch length of ribbon
White ornament
Needle

HERE'S HOW
1 Enlarge, trace, and cut out the pattern. Trace the pattern onto fleece for front and back and cut out.
2 If your fleece has a right side, place the right sides together and sew the main portion of the stocking, down the sides and around the bottom leaving the top opening unsewn. Clip the rounded corners and the pointed toe; turn.
3 Sew the white cuff pieces together. Place the cuff inside the sewn body of the stocking, aligning the top edges. Line up the front and back seams of the cuff to the colored stocking front and back seams. Stretch the colored stocking portion slightly to fit cuff, as it is slightly smaller than the cuff. Sew the layers together around the edge. Trim the threads; turn the cuff outward. Stitch a ribbon hanger to the upper corner of the stocking.
4 Tie a ribbon to a white ornament. With needle and thread, sew ribbon underneath white cuff.

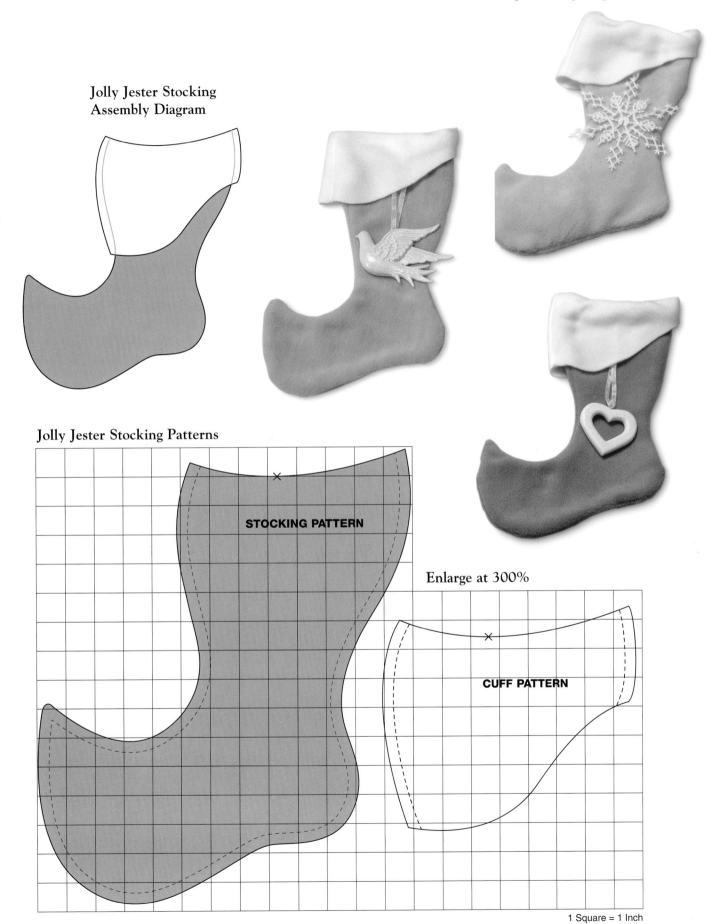

Jolly Jester Stocking
Assembly Diagram

Jolly Jester Stocking Patterns

STOCKING PATTERN

Enlarge at 300%

CUFF PATTERN

1 Square = 1 Inch

woodland
holiday

Subtle colors, simple shapes, and woodsy items from Mother Nature inspire naturally beautiful decor.

Whether decorating a cabin or your comfortable urban home, these projects add rustic appeal. Easy-to-manage sheets of embossing aluminum and copper bring dimension to evergreens as **Stars of Silver** and **Copper Reindeer.** The **Pretty Patched Throw,** *opposite*, is made of hand-embroidered wool to ward off a wintry chill. Instructions and patterns are on *pages 34–35*.

Make your tree as delightful as a walk in the woods with ornaments inspired by trees. Drape clear holiday ornaments with leaves edged in beads to make **Frosted Fallen Leaves,** *opposite*. Create **Sequined Pinecones** as a sparkling version of one of Mother Nature's most curious creations. Nestled naturally in the branches of the Christmas tree, **Frosted Bird Nests** with clay eggs offer hope of new life. Instructions are on *pages 35–36*.

Bursts of color, whether in an arrangement of greenery or on a stocking cuff, entice both eyes and senses. Put together a bountiful **Berries and Peels Perfection** wall piece using brilliant red cranberries and orange peels. To showcase a sampling of delicate hand stitches, sew up a **Stitches-and-Strips Stocking,** *opposite*. You'll be proud to hang this vintage-looking stocking from your mantel in Santa's honor. Instructions and patterns are on *pages 36–37*.

Unusual combinations of materials establish interesting texture and appeal. **Nature's Presentation,** *opposite,* gives pillar candles a new look wrapped with twigs, leaves, berries, and fibers. To brighten an entryway, craft a **Northwoods Swag** from evergreen cuttings, kumquats, berries, and miniature squash. Instructions are on *page 38*.

Simplicity is key to this elegant **Dancing Snowflake Wreath,** *opposite*, that features a glistening ornament center stage. If you enjoy candle making, **Hand-Dipped Tapers** are perfect for your own home and for gifts. To craft a natural candleholder, drill a birch log in whatever length you desire. Instructions are on *page 39*.

Stars of Silver

shown on page 24

WHAT YOU NEED

Tracing paper
Pencil; embossing tool
Medium-weight aluminum metal
 sheet, such as Art Emboss
Scissors; ruler
$\frac{1}{16}$-inch hole punch
Jump ring
Needlenose pliers
$\frac{1}{8}$- to $\frac{1}{4}$-inch-wide satin ribbon

HERE'S HOW

1 Enlarge and trace the pattern, *below,* onto tracing paper. Use the embossing tool to trace it onto a section of the metal sheet. Slowly cut out the traced star shape. (Tip: Cut out each point from the outside in. The metal sheet will rip if you rotate the scissors in

Star Pattern
Enlarge at 175%

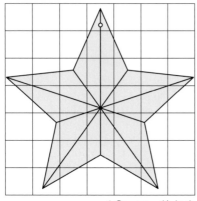

1 Square = $\frac{1}{2}$ Inch

between each point.) Use the embossing tool to make round dots around the star edges.

2 Use a ruler as a guide to help position the fold lines. Place the ruler down the center of each point. Use the embossing tool to trace a line along the ruler edge. Each line should span from the star tip to the star center. Flip the star over and use the ruler to make a second set of fold lines. This time, each line should span from the outside edge between each point to the star center. Use your fingertips to finish shaping the star by pushing up the center lines along each star point and pushing down on the lines between the points.

3 Punch a hole in one of the star points. Open the jump ring laterally and thread it through the hole. Use the pliers to pinch the jump ring closed. Thread a length of hanging ribbon through the jump ring, bring the ends together and tie them in an overhand knot.

Copper Reindeer

shown on page 24

WHAT YOU NEED

Tracing paper; pencil
Embossing tool; scissors
Medium-weight copper metal
 sheet, such as Art Emboss
$\frac{1}{16}$-inch hole punch
Paintbrush with small handle
Jump ring; needlenose pliers
$\frac{1}{8}$- to $\frac{1}{4}$-inch-wide satin ribbon

HERE'S HOW

1 Enlarge and trace the pattern, *right,* onto tracing paper. Use the embossing tool to trace it onto a section of the metal sheet. Slowly cut out the traced reindeer shape. (Tip: Cut out each point from the outside in. The metal sheet will rip if you rotate the scissors in between each point.)

2 Punch one hole in the reindeer head to make his eye and another hole at the shoulder for hanging.

3 Use the narrow handle end of the paintbrush to shape the reindeer. Working on one section at a time, position the handle end in the center of the head and each leg. Wrap the metal sides around the handle, then slide out the handle. From the underside, the finished shaped head and legs appear as narrow cylinders. The antler points and tail are simply curled around the handle to add dimension.

4 Open the jump ring laterally and thread it through the hole in the reindeer's shoulders. Use the pliers to pinch the jump ring closed. Thread a length of hanging ribbon through the jump ring; bring the ends together, and tie them in an overhand knot.

Deer Pattern
Enlarge at 175%

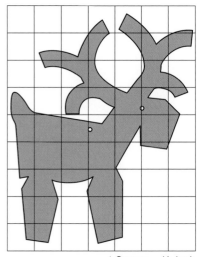

1 Square = $\frac{1}{2}$ Inch

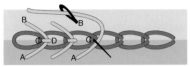

Step 1 | Step 2
Lazy Daisy Stitch

Chain Stitch with
Fly Stitch Accent

Chain Stitch

Pretty Patched Throw

shown on page 25

Finished size is 60×84 inches.

WHAT YOU NEED

Scissors; ruler; ¾ yard of 54- to
60-inch-wide wool fabrics in
7 different prints or colors
Sewing machine; thread; iron
Assorted colors of wool
needlepoint yarn and perle
cotton
Embroidery needle
5 yards of 45-inch-wide flannel
fabric for back

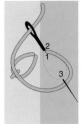

Featherstitch   French Knot

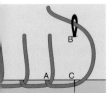

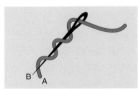

Blanket Stitch   Closed Blanket Stitch

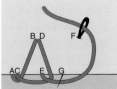

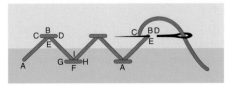

Chevron Stitch

HERE'S HOW

1 Cut 35 pieces of wool fabric, each
12½ inches square.

2 Piece the wool squares together,
right sides facing, using a ¼-inch seam.
Piece together five squares across and
seven squares down. Press the seams in
one direction.

3 With wool yarn and perle cotton,
embroider across seam lines between
the squares. Work embroidery stitches,
such as featherstitches, cross-stitches,
blanket stitches, French knots, lazy
daisy stitches, Chevron, chain stitches,
and the blanket-stitches as shown
at *left*.

4 For back cut and piece flannel fabric
the same size as the pieced front. Stitch
front to back, leaving an opening for
turning. Trim corners and turn to right
side. Stitch the opening closed. Press
the edge.

5 Topstitch around the outside edge
through all layers. Tie the throw with
needlepoint yarn where seams meet at
corners of squares.

Frosted Fallen Leaves

shown on page 26

WHAT YOU NEED

Glass ball ornaments
Artificial fall-color oak leaves
Scissors
Thick white crafts glue; glue brush
Clear mini glass marbles
Decoupage medium; Liquid Beadz
¼-inch-wide ocher satin ribbon

HERE'S HOW

1 Remove the metal cap and hanger
from each of the glass ornaments and
temporarily set them aside.

2 Cut several oak leaves from the
stems. Brush glue onto the underside of
one of the leaves and wrap the leaf glue
side down around the ball. Hold the
newly attached leaf in your cupped
hand for a minute as the glue begins to
set. Repeat the process with each of two
remaining leaves, overlapping portions
while allowing the clear glass to remain
visible. If necessary, apply more glue
under the leaf tips so they lay flat
against the glass; let dry overnight.

3 Pour about two tablespoons of clear
glass mini marbles into the ball, pouring
directly from the plastic bag packaging.
Replace the cap and hanger on the top
of the ball.

4 Brush a protective coat of decoupage
medium over the oak leaves. Let the
decoupage medium dry. Embellish the
leaves with decorative accents of Liquid
Beadz, concentrating on the edges of
the leaves especially around the base of
the hanger. Let dry.

5 Thread an ocher hanging ribbon
through the hanger, and tie the ends
together in an overhand knot.

Sequined Pinecones

shown on page 27

WHAT YOU NEED

Bell-shape dylite (avoid other
plastic foams as they will not
hold the pins); scissors
Seed and E glass beads
Small and large round gold and
silver sequins
¾-inch-long straight pins
Ribbon

HERE'S HOW

1 An inverted bell shape is similar to a
pinecone shape. To improve it, use
scissors to trim off the outside bell rim
(which is now at the top) and narrow
the rounded end (which is now at the
base) so that it is pointed.
2 Beginning at the base of the
pinecone, thread a seed bead followed
by a small sequin onto a pin; firmly
press it into the dylite. Continue adding
sequined pins so they spiral up the base
until the bottom quarter of the
pinecone is completely covered. As you
work your way up the pinecone,
continue using seed beads but pierce
the pin through the top of the small
sequin instead of its center hole. At the
halfway point switch to threading E
beads and large sequins onto the pins.
Continue piercing the pins through the
top of the sequins instead of using their
center holes until the entire dylite base
is concealed with sequins.
3 Crown the finished pinecone by
pinning on a decorative bow and
hanging loop into the center top.

Frosted Bird Nests

shown on page 27

WHAT YOU NEED

Thick white crafts glue
Twig nests
Green moss
Polymer clay, such as Sculpey, in
light blue, ivory, and tan
Glass and bead glue, such as
Aleene's Platinum Bond
Liquid Beadz
⅛-inch-wide wired gold ribbon
Scissors; ruler

HERE'S HOW

1 Apply crafts glue to the inside of the
twig nest. Press green moss over the glue
to line the nest. Brush away any loose
moss from the work surface before
working with the clay.
2 Blend light blue, ivory, and tan clay
together so that the colors are partially
integrated. Roll this multicolored clay
into rounded eggs that are about the
length of an almond. Make three eggs
for each nest. Bake the eggs according
to the package instructions. Let cool.
3 Use glass and bead glue to anchor the
eggs inside the nest. Let dry.
4 Brush Liquid Beadz along the twigs
and the rim of the nest. Let dry.
5 For hanging ribbons, cut three 6-inch
lengths of wired gold ribbon and tie a
ribbon end to each of the three twigs.
Bring other ribbon ends together above
the nest and tie them in an overhand
knot. Tie a separate length of ribbon in
a decorative bow around one of the
twigs alongside the nest.

Berries and Peels Perfection

shown on page 28

WHAT YOU NEED

Oranges; grapefruit knife
1½-inch star-shape cookie cutter
Tapestry needle
Waxed beading cord;
fresh cranberries
8-inch-long food
skewers
Metal buckets
Greens
Plaid ribbon
Scissors

HERE'S HOW

1 *For the stars* cut off ½
inch from each end of
orange. Cut the orange
in half lengthwise.
Use a grapefruit knife
to remove the peel. Use
a star-shape cookie cutter to
cut shapes in the peel, cutting
about four to six stars from
each orange.
2 *For the garland* thread needle with
waxed beading cord and string through
five cranberries then through the top of
an orange peel star. Repeat until the
desired length is achieved.
3 *For the picks* slide cranberries onto
skewer, leaving room at the tip for an
orange star.
4 To hang on a wall, fill metal buckets
with greens, tuck in cranberry-orange
picks, and finish with a plaid bow.

Stitches-and-Strips Stocking

shown on page 29

The stocking is 20½ inches long.

WHAT YOU NEED

Tracing paper; pencil

Scissors

⅝ yard of dark red wool fabric

Fusible transweb paper

⅝ yard of lining fabric

Assorted wool fabrics

Assorted colors of wool
  needlepoint yarn and perle
  cotton; sewing machine

Embroidery needle

Batting; thread; ruler

HERE'S HOW

1 Enlarge and trace the stocking and heel patterns, *right*.

2 Cut stocking front and back from red wool fabric, allowing for a ¼ inch seam allowance. Repeat for lining.

3 For the stocking heel trace the shape onto transweb paper according to manufacturer's directions. Fuse to an appropriate size piece of plaid wool, cut out, and fuse to stocking.

4 Embellish the rounded curve of the heel with the desired embroidery stitches as shown on *page 35*.

5 Line the stocking front with batting trimmed even with stocking shape. With right sides facing, stitch the stocking front to back except at top

edge. Trim and clip seam allowance. Turn to right side.

6 For the cuff cut wool fabric rectangles 7½ inches long and varying widths. Stitch the rectangles together lengthwise using a ¼-inch seam. Piece a 19-inch-long section.

7 Cut a piece of lining fabric the same size as the pieced cuff. Stitch the lining to the pieced cuff along bottom edge. Stitch side seams of cuff and lining, adjusting to fit top opening of the stocking. Trim seam allowance. Press the cuff lining to the wrong side of the pieced cuff. Baste raw edges of lined cuff to top of the stocking.

8 For fabric loop cut a 1½×6-inch piece of fabric. Press the raw edges lengthwise into the center. Press in half lengthwise again and stitch. Fold in half crosswise and stitch in place.

9 Stitch lining pieces together, leaving an opening for turning. Slip stocking into lining with right sides facing and matching seams. Stitch around top edge. Trim and clip seam.

10 Pull stocking through opening in lining. Stitch opening closed. Smooth and press lining to inside of stocking.

11 Decorate the cuff seams with embroidery stitches.

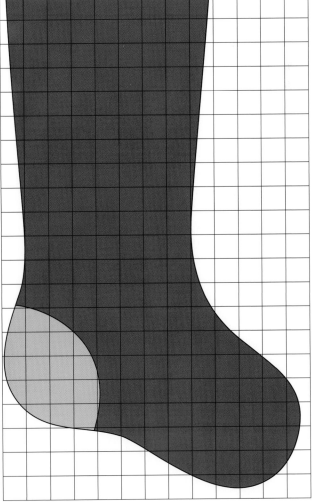

Stitches-and-Strips Stocking Pattern

Enlarge at 400%

1 Square = 1 Inch

Nature's Presentation

shown on page 30

WHAT YOU NEED

   Greenery
   Twigs
   Gilded seedpods
   Scissors
   Pillar candles
   Floral tape or a rubber band
   Raffia or ribbon
   Straight pins

HERE'S HOW

1 Decide which natural materials will be used to decorate each candle. Cut the lengths of the greenery, twigs, or seedpods, if necessary, to be shorter than the candle.
2 Use floral tape or a rubber band to hold the natural items in place around the base of the candle.
3 Tie raffia or ribbon over the floral tape or rubber band. Trim the ribbon ends if desired.
4 For the pod-covered candle pin on the pods in a pattern or randomly.

Note: *Never leave burning candles unattended.*

Northwoods Swag

shown on page 31

WHAT YOU NEED

   ¼-inch-diameter dowels
   Yardstick
   Saw
   Green floral wire
   Evergreen cuttings
   Hot-glue gun and glue sticks
   Kumquats
   Blueberries
   Raspberries
   Miniature squash

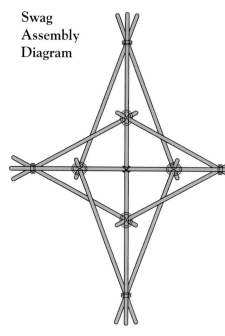

Swag Assembly Diagram

HERE'S HOW

1 Cut 32- and 24-inch lengths of dowel for the cross. For the vertical angled pieces, cut four 18-inch lengths. For the horizontal angled pieces, cut four 15-inch lengths. Arrange the dowels as shown, *above*. Secure the intersections with wire.
2 Cover the form with evergreen cuttings, attaching pieces securely with floral wire.
3 Hot-glue the fruits as desired in a border around the swag, adding more evergreens if needed.

Note: *The berries in this swag will last a few days outside in cold weather. Citrus fruits and squash will last longer. Use artificial fruits and berries for a longer-lasting wreath.*

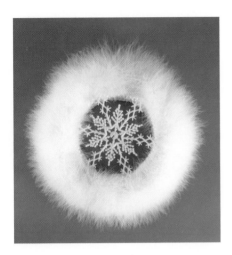

Dancing Snowflake Wreath

shown on page 32

WHAT YOU NEED

- White braid trim
- Tape, optional
- Straight pins
- Scissors
- Plastic foam wreath form
- White feather boa
- Hot-glue gun and glue sticks
- White snowflake ornament to fit wreath center

HERE'S HOW

1 If the braid is the kind that will fray easily, wrap a small piece of clear tape around the edge to secure it. Pin one end of white braid onto inside of wreath form. Continue to wind the braid and pin in place until the inner circle is completely covered. Apply another small piece of tape to the end to be trimmed off. Cut off the end, cutting through the braid and the tape. Pin in place onto wreath form.

2 Pin one end of feather boa onto outside edge of wreath form. Continue to wrap the boa around wreath form, pinning in place every 2 to 3 inches until form is completely covered.

3 Hot-glue the snowflake in the center.

Hand-Dipped Tapers

shown on page 33

WHAT YOU NEED

- Old saucepan and can
- New block of candle wax or old candles; sharp knife
- Heat source, such as a stove or hot plate (do not use a microwave)
- Candle coloring and scent, optional
- Waxed paper; pot holder
- Bowl or deep pan of ice water
- Candle wicking; scissors; ruler

HERE'S HOW

Note: *Candle wax comes in big clear no-color slabs or sometimes in smaller colored chunks. If you are starting with large pieces, cut them into smaller chunks (about ½- to 1-inch squares) with a knife. Put the chunks into the old can. You also can use old candles cut into chunks.*

1 Fill the saucepan about half full of water. Put the can of candle wax chunks in the saucepan of water. Place the pan on the stove. The water will boil and melt the wax in the can. Don't let the water boil too hard. It should just simmer and slowly melt the wax. NEVER put the wax directly on the stove or in the microwave. It is very flammable.

2 After the wax melts, add coloring or scent desired. Turn off stove. Cover the work area with waxed paper. Using a pot holder, lift the can out of the water and onto the waxed paper. Put the bowl of ice water beside the can of wax.

3 Cut a length of candle wicking, approximately 16 inches, to make two candles at a time. The length can vary a lot. Extra is needed to hold onto when dipping the candles. Holding the wicking between the two ends, dip each end into the wax and take out, keeping the two candles separated.

4 Dip each end of the waxed wicking into the ice water. The wax will cool quickly and start to build up on the wicking. Repeat back and forth quickly between wax and water. The ice water will set the wax almost immediately so you can move back and forth from the can to the bowl very quickly.

5 After the wax has built up enough, (about four or five times), alternate and have one side in wax while the other side is in the water. As the candles get bigger, this will keep them from sticking together.

6 When the candles are the desired size, hang them over a chair back or rack to dry. When they are completely dry (this will only take a few minutes), cut them apart. Slice off the bottom of the base to even it off so it will fit more easily into a candleholder.

Note: *Because the bases of hand-dipped candles are not flat, be sure the candles are level and secure before lighting them. You may hear a popping sound when they are lit. This is just a little water that might be trapped between layers. Never leave burning candles unattended.*

christmas
goodies

Here's a delectable selection of party appetizers, sippers, cookies, and desserts to make this year's gatherings your merriest ever!

An almond-imbued take on the good old-fashioned sugar cookie, **Mitten Cookies,** *opposite*, say "celebrate the season" in the sweetest of ways. **Triple Treat Crème de Menthe Bars,** *below*, bring three lavish layers no one can refuse: a stunning nut-and-coconut crust, a creamy mint-infused layer, and a sheen of semisweet chocolate. Recipes are on *page 47*.

Lemon-Basil Cheese Ball, *below*, will taste great at one of your holiday get-togethers, but remember it for gift-giving too. Present it on a pedestal right before Christmas—the recipient will appreciate receiving such a festive treat to help round out a holiday spread. A great kickoff to a holiday sledding party, **Fire and Ice Nut Mix,** *opposite*, combines cashews spiced with soy sauce and cayenne pepper and buttery, maple-toasted pecans. Recipes are on *page 48*.

The bright color and festive sparkle of **Mulled Cranberry Drink,** *opposite*, will catch everyone's attention right away. Love at first sip will follow. Party-goers will go wild for **Cheesy Sausage and Spinach Dip** and **Mexican-Style Meatballs and Smokies,** *center*. **Pecan Crunch Orange and Pumpkin Pie,** *below*, dresses up a classic for the holiday. Recipes are on *pages 48–50*.

Spiced Bread Pudding with Cranberry Maple Sauce, *left*, is an old-fashioned dessert with a holiday-special angle. Decorate Chocolate-Peppermint Fantasy Cake, *below*, to look like a gift box, because indeed, there is a surprise inside: a luscious Peppermint Fudge Filling. Recipes are on *pages 50–51*.

Mitten Cookies

shown on page 40

WHAT YOU NEED

1½	cups butter, softened
1⅔	cups granulated sugar
2	teaspoons baking powder
½	teaspoon salt
2	eggs
¼	cup buttermilk
½	teaspoon vanilla
⅓	cup ground toasted almonds
4	cups all-purpose flour
	Coarse colored sugars

HERE'S HOW

1 In a large bowl beat butter with an electric mixer on medium to high speed for 30 seconds. Add granulated sugar, baking powder, and salt. Beat until combined, scraping sides of bowl occasionally. Beat in eggs, buttermilk, and vanilla until combined. Beat in ground almonds and as much of the flour as you can with the mixer. Using a wooden spoon, stir in any remaining flour. Cover and chill dough about 2 hours or until easy to handle.

2 Using ⅓ cup dough for each cookie, shape dough into balls. Place 3½ inches apart on an ungreased cookie sheet. Cover with plastic wrap and flatten with hand or bottom of a pie plate to 4- to 5-inch rounds. Place a mitten cookie cutter or a stencil* on top of cookie; sprinkle colored sugar inside the cutter or stencil. Remove and repeat with remaining cookies.

3 Bake in a 375°F oven about 14 minutes or until edges are firm and bottoms are brown. Cool on cookie sheet for 2 to 3 minutes. Transfer cookies to a wire rack and let cool. Makes 16 large cookies.

To Store: Place in layers separated by waxed paper in an airtight container. Store at room temperature up to 3 days or freeze up to 3 months.

***Mitten Stencil:** Draw a mitten shape about 3 inches long on heavy cardboard or on the back of a stiff paper plate. Cut out mitten with a sharp knife or scissors.

Triple Treat Crème de Menthe Bars

shown on page 41

WHAT YOU NEED

2	cups graham cracker crumbs
1½	cups finely chopped walnuts
1	cup shredded coconut
¾	cup butter,* melted
½	cup powdered sugar
¼	cup unsweetened cocoa powder
1	teaspoon vanilla
2	cups powdered sugar
½	cup butter,* melted
3	tablespoons green crème de menthe liqueur
½	teaspoon vanilla
1	12-ounce package (2 cups) semisweet chocolate pieces
½	cup butter*

HERE'S HOW

1 For crust, line a 13×9×2-inch baking pan with foil, extending edges over sides. In a large bowl stir together graham cracker crumbs, walnuts, coconut, the ¾ cup melted butter, the ½ cup powdered sugar, the cocoa powder, and the 1 teaspoon vanilla until well combined. Press mixture into the bottom of the prepared pan. Chill about 1 hour or until firm.

2 For crème de menthe layer, in a large mixing bowl combine the 2 cups powdered sugar, the ½ cup melted butter, the crème de menthe, and the ½ teaspoon vanilla. Beat with an electric mixer on medium speed until smooth. Spread mixture evenly over crust. Chill about 30 minutes or until firm.

3 For chocolate layer, in a small saucepan combine the chocolate pieces and the ½ cup butter. Cook and stir over medium-low heat just until melted. Remove from heat; cool slightly. Spread melted chocolate evenly over the crème de menthe layer. Chill about 1 hour or until chocolate sets.

4 Carefully lift bars out of pan using edges of foil. Peel off foil and transfer bars to a cutting board. Using a large thin-bladed knife, cut down into bars to make small squares or cut into triangles. Makes 6 dozen bars.

To Store: Place in layers separated by waxed paper in an airtight container. Store in the refrigerator up to 3 days or freeze up to 1 month.

***Note:** Make sure you use real butter in this recipe.

Fire and Ice Nut Mix

shown on page 43

WHAT YOU NEED

1½	pounds lightly salted cashews (4½ cups)
¾	teaspoon cayenne pepper
3	tablespoons soy sauce or Indonesian sauce
3	tablespoons honey
¾	cup pure maple syrup
4	teaspoons butter, melted
1½	pounds pecan halves (6 cups)

HERE'S HOW

1 For the "fire" nuts, line two 15×10×1-inch baking pans with foil. Grease foil; set aside. In a food processor or blender, place 1½ cups of the cashews. Cover and process or blend until finely ground. Stir together ground cashews and cayenne pepper. In a large bowl stir together soy sauce and honey. Add remaining whole cashews, stirring to coat. Add ground cashew mixture and stir well. Spread mixture in the prepared pans. Bake in a 350°F oven for 25 to 30 minutes if using soy sauce (or 15 to 20 minutes if using Indonesian sauce) or until browned, stirring two or three times. Cool completely. Break the nuts into pieces.

2 For the "ice" nuts, line the same baking pans with new foil. Grease foil; set aside. In a large bowl stir together maple syrup and melted butter. Add pecans, tossing to coat. Spread pecans

in the prepared pans. Bake in the 350°F oven 20 minutes, stirring twice. Cool completely. To serve, combine both types of nuts in a bowl. Store in an airtight container. Makes 13 cups.

Lemon-Basil Cheese Ball

shown on page 42

WHAT YOU NEED

1	8-ounce carton mascarpone cheese
3	tablespoons finely chopped pistachio nuts or toasted almonds
2	tablespoons finely snipped fresh basil
1	tablespoon finely shredded lemon peel
1	cup shredded Gruyère cheese (4 ounces)
	Assorted crackers
	Lemon peel slices (optional)
	Basil sprig (optional)

HERE'S HOW

1 Stir together mascarpone, nuts, basil, peel, and ⅛ teaspoon black pepper. Stir in Gruyère. Line a small bowl with plastic wrap. Transfer mixture to bowl, pressing firmly into bowl. Cover; chill 3 hours or until firm. (Can be refrigerated up to 3 days.) To serve, unmold onto a plate; remove plastic wrap. Serve with crackers. If desired, garnish with lemon peel slices and basil sprig. Serves 12.

Mulled Cranberry Drink

shown on page 44

WHAT YOU NEED

5	cups cranberry juice cocktail
1½	cups fresh cranberries (6 ounces)
⅓	cup honey
¼	cup crystallized ginger, chopped
1	teaspoon cardamom pods or ¼ teaspoon ground cardamom
½	teaspoon whole black pepper, cracked
1	vanilla bean, split

HERE'S HOW

1 In a large saucepan stir together all ingredients. Heat over medium heat until mixture boils and cranberry skins pop. Remove from heat. Cover and let stand for 5 minutes. Strain and discard solids. Serve warm.* Makes 8 to 10 servings (about 4 ounces each). If desired, serve with a vanilla bean as a stirrer.

*Test Kitchen Tip: Cover and chill any leftovers. Reheat or, if desired, serve over ice.

Cheesy Sausage and Spinach Dip

shown on pages 44-45

WHAT YOU NEED

8	ounces bulk sweet or hot Italian sausage
½	cup chopped onion
½	cup chopped red sweet pepper
2	cloves garlic, minced
2	8-ounce packages reduced-fat cream cheese (Neufchâtel), softened
1½	cups finely shredded Parmesan or Romano cheese
¼	cup milk
¼	cup mayonnaise
¼	cup light dairy sour cream
2	cups chopped fresh spinach leaves
⅓	cup mild banana pepper rings, drained and chopped Crostini, bagel chips, blue corn tortilla chips, or sliced baguette-style French bread

HERE'S HOW

1 In a large skillet cook sausage, onion, sweet pepper, and garlic until sausage is brown, stirring often. Drain off fat. Set sausage mixture aside to let cool.

2 In a large bowl stir together cream cheese, Parmesan cheese, milk, mayonnaise, and sour cream. Add sausage mixture, spinach, and banana peppers; gently stir to combine. Spread mixture into a 9-inch fluted quiche dish or deep-dish pie plate.

3 Bake in a 350°F oven about 30 minutes or until bubbly. Serve with crostini, bagel chips, blue corn tortilla chips, or French bread. Makes 5 cups (twenty ¼-cup servings).

To Make Ahead: Prepare as directed through Step 2. Cover and chill for up to 24 hours. Uncover and bake about 40 minutes or until heated through.

Mexican-Style Meatballs and Smokies

shown on page 45

WHAT YOU NEED

1	slightly beaten egg
¼	cup fine dry bread crumbs
¼	cup finely chopped onion
2	tablespoons snipped fresh cilantro
3	cloves garlic, minced
½	teaspoon salt
8	ounces lean ground beef
8	ounces chorizo (casing removed, if necessary)
1	16-ounce jar salsa
1	12-ounce jar chili sauce
1	16-ounce package small fully cooked smoked sausage links

HERE'S HOW

1 In a medium bowl combine egg, bread crumbs, onion, cilantro, garlic, and salt. Add the ground beef and chorizo; mix well. Shape into 50 meatballs.

2 Place meatballs in 15×10×1-inch baking pan. Bake in a 350°F oven about 15 minutes or until no longer pink inside. Drain meatballs.

3 In a large saucepan stir together salsa and chili sauce. Stir in baked meatballs and smoked sausage links. Cook over medium-high heat until heated through, stirring occasionally. Serve immediately or keep warm in 3½- to 4-quart slow cooker on low-heat setting for up to 2 hours. Makes 25 servings (about 100 pieces).

christmas goodies

Pecan Crunch Orange and Pumpkin Pie

shown on page 45

WHAT YOU NEED

1	recipe Orange Pastry
1	15-ounce can pumpkin
1	5-ounce can (⅔ cup) evaporated milk
2	slightly beaten eggs
⅔	cup granulated sugar
2½	teaspoons finely shredded orange peel (divided use)
1½	teaspoons pumpkin pie spice
½	cup packed brown sugar
½	cup chopped pecans
2	tablespoons all-purpose flour
2	tablespoons butter, softened
1	recipe Orange-Spiked Whipped Cream (optional)

HERE'S HOW

1 Prepare Orange Pastry. On a lightly floured surface, use your hands to slightly flatten dough. Roll dough from center to edges into a 12-inch circle. To transfer pastry, wrap it around the rolling pin. Unroll pastry into a 9-inch pie plate without stretching it. Trim pastry to ½ inch beyond edge of pie plate. Fold under extra pastry. Crimp edge as desired. Set aside.

2 Stir together pumpkin, evaporated milk, and eggs. Stir in granulated sugar, 1½ teaspoons of the orange peel, the pie spice, and ½ teaspoon salt. Pour into pastry-lined plate. To prevent overbrowning, cover edge of pie with foil. Bake in a 375°F oven for 25 minutes.

3 Meanwhile, in a medium bowl stir together the brown sugar, pecans, flour, butter, and the remaining 1 teaspoon orange peel until combined. Remove foil from pie. Sprinkle brown sugar mixture over top of pie. Bake for 20 minutes more. Cool completely on a wire rack before serving. If desired, serve with Orange-Spiked Whipped Cream. Makes 8 servings.

Orange Pastry: In a medium bowl stir together 1¼ cups all-purpose flour, 1 tablespoon granulated sugar, 1½ teaspoons finely shredded orange peel, and ¼ teaspoon salt. Using a pastry blender, cut in ⅓ cup butter-flavored shortening until pieces are pea-size. Sprinkle 1 tablespoon cold water over part of the flour mixture; gently toss with a fork. Push moistened dough to the side of the bowl. Repeat moistening flour mixture, using 1 tablespoon of water at a time (4 to 5 tablespoons total), until all flour mixture is moistened. Form dough into a ball.

Orange-Spiked Whipped Cream: In a chilled mixing bowl, beat 1 cup whipping cream, 2 tablespoons granulated sugar, and 1 tablespoon orange liqueur with an electric mixer on medium speed until soft peaks form.

Spiced Bread Pudding with Cranberry-Maple Sauce

shown on page 46

WHAT YOU NEED

6	cups dry rich egg bread cubes, such as challah or brioche*
½	cup pecan pieces, toasted
4	eggs
2	cups half-and-half or light cream
⅔	cup packed brown sugar
2	tablespoons molasses
½	teaspoon ground cinnamon
¼	teaspoon salt
¼	teaspoon ground ginger
¼	teaspoon ground nutmeg
1	recipe Cranberry-Maple Sauce
	Sweetened whipped cream (optional)

HERE'S HOW

1 Lightly grease a 2-quart square baking dish. Spread bread cubes in the bottom of the dish. Sprinkle with pecans. Set aside.

2 In a large mixing bowl, use a rotary beater or wire whisk to beat together the eggs, half-and-half, brown sugar, molasses, cinnamon, salt, ginger, and nutmeg. Slowly pour mixture over bread cubes and pecans in dish. Press bread cubes down lightly with back of a large spoon to completely soak.

50

christmas goodies

3 Bake, uncovered, in a 350°F oven for 35 to 40 minutes or until puffed and a knife inserted near the center comes out clean. Serve warm with Cranberry-Maple Sauce and, if desired, sweetened whipped cream. Makes 8 servings.

Cranberry-Maple Sauce: In a small saucepan combine 1 cup fresh cranberries and ⅓ cup cranberry juice. Bring to boiling; reduce heat. Cook, uncovered, about 2 minutes or until cranberries pop, stirring occasionally. Stir in ½ cup pure maple syrup. Bring to boiling; boil gently for 10 minutes. Cool slightly before serving.

*Note: To dry bread cubes, spread 6 cups bread cubes (6 to 7 ounces) in a shallow baking pan. Bake in a 300°F oven for 10 to 15 minutes or until bread cubes are dry, stirring twice; cool.

Chocolate-Peppermint Fantasy Cake

Decorate with candy canes, as shown. Or top with alternating strips of bittersweet chocolate curls and finely chopped peppermint sticks, candy canes, or other hard peppermint candies. Shown on page 46.

WHAT YOU NEED

¾ cup butter, softened
3 eggs
2 cups all-purpose flour
¾ cup unsweetened cocoa powder
1 teaspoon baking soda
¾ teaspoon baking powder
½ teaspoon salt
2 cups sugar
2 teaspoons vanilla
1½ cups milk
⅓ cup finely chopped peppermint sticks, candy canes, or other hard peppermint candies
1 recipe Peppermint Fudge Filling and Chocolate Whipped Cream Frosting
15 to 20 candy canes, broken into desired lengths (optional)

HERE'S HOW

1 Allow butter and eggs to stand at room temperature for 30 minutes. Meanwhile, lightly grease bottoms of two 8×8×2-inch square cake pans. Line bottoms of pans with waxed paper. Grease and lightly flour bottoms and sides of pans. Set aside. In a medium bowl stir together flour, cocoa powder, baking soda, baking powder, and salt. Set aside.

2 In a large mixing bowl beat butter with an electric mixer on medium to high speed for 30 seconds. Gradually add sugar, about ¼ cup at a time, beating on medium speed until well combined (3 to 4 minutes). Scrape sides of bowl; continue beating on medium speed for 2 minutes more. Add eggs 1 at a time, beating after each addition (about 1 minute total). Beat in vanilla.

3 Alternately add flour mixture and milk to butter mixture, beating on low speed after each addition just until combined. Beat on medium to high speed for 20 seconds more. Spread batter evenly into prepared pans.

4 Bake in a 350°F oven for 35 to 40 minutes or until a toothpick inserted near centers comes out clean. Cool in pans for 10 minutes. Remove from pans. Peel off waxed paper. Cool cakes thoroughly on wire racks.

5 To assemble, place a cake layer on a serving plate. Stir the ⅓ cup finely chopped peppermint sticks into the Peppermint Fudge Filling. Spread the filling evenly over the cake. Top with the remaining cake layer. Spread Chocolate Whipped Cream Frosting over top and sides of cake. If desired, decorate top of cake with candy canes to resemble ribbons and a bow on top of cake, as shown *left*. Cover and chill up to 4 hours. Makes 12 to 16 servings.

Peppermint Fudge Filling and Chocolate Whipped Cream Frosting: In a medium saucepan heat and stir 1 cup whipping cream and ¼ cup butter over medium heat until butter melts. Remove from heat. Add 1 pound chopped bittersweet chocolate; let stand, uncovered, for 5 minutes. Stir mixture until smooth. For the Peppermint Fudge Filling, transfer 1¼ cups of the chocolate mixture to a small bowl. Stir 1 tablespoon peppermint schnapps or ½ teaspoon peppermint extract into chocolate mixture in bowl. Cover and chill for 1 to 2 hours, stirring occasionally, or until mixture is cold. Let remaining chocolate mixture in saucepan cool to room temperature.

For the Chocolate Whipped Cream Frosting, in a large chilled mixing bowl, beat 2 cups whipping cream with an electric mixer on medium speed until soft peaks form. Fold in half of the remaining chocolate mixture at a time.

51

santas & snowmen

Whether you fancy snowmen with their well-rounded personalities or endearing Santas in all shapes and sizes, this chapter sets your heart aglow with the warmth and wonder they represent.

Perched on a mantel or tucked in a couch corner, grinning snowmen and Santas set a jolly mood. The **Canvas Characters,** *opposite,* can be posed, ready for holiday hugs. To toss Christmas flair on a couch or chair, stitch up a **Snow Lady Sue Pillow** from so-soft fleece. Instructions and patterns are on *pages 60–62.*

If there were a prize for the best dressed in Jack Frost's wonderland, these characters would offer stiff competition. The soft **Chenille Santa Snow Gal,** *opposite,* dons accessories stitched from decorator fabrics in traditional maroon and green. The small **Smiling Snowmen** ornaments, made of clay and sticks, are clad in brighter tones dusted with glitter. Arrange these fellows on a table or shelf or thread them with ribbon to hang from the tree. Instructions and patterns are on *pages 62–64.*

Whether wide-smile snowmen or gentle St. Nicks, these guys melt your heart with holiday joy. The **Snow Fella Ornaments** are created using glass paint and simple patterns. **Jolly Lollipops,** made of coordinating clays, make a playful combination. The fleece **Snuggle-Up Santa Throw** will warm cold toes after playing in the snow. Instructions and patterns are on *pages 64–68.*

Snowmen are welcome signs of winter and this happy group
bodes well for the season. The **Carefree Characters,** *opposite,* are
jovial creations that start with a ball ornament and are adorned
with sock hats and wire noses. **Front Door Frosty** is a cleverly
disguised cake pan touting dimensional accents that ring in
smiles at every opening. Instructions are on *page 69.*

Canvas Characters

shown on page 52

WHAT YOU NEED

Tracing paper; pencil

Scissors

¼ yard of heavyweight white
cotton fabric; straight pins

6 standard chenille stems

White thread; sewing machine

Plastic pellets; fiberfill

White acrylic paint

¼- to ½-inch flat paintbrush

Fine paintbrush

2 white wide chenille stems

Hot-glue gun and glue sticks

FOR THE SNOWMAN

1 white and 2 light blue miniature
pom-poms

Acrylic paint in light blue, dark
blue, orange, red, and black

FOR THE SANTA

Acrylic paints in red, light green,
black, gray, and pink

1 small white pom-pom

2 small red pom-poms

HERE'S HOW

1 Enlarge and trace the patterns, *opposite*, onto tracing paper; cut out. Trace around patterns onto the white fabric. It is unnecessary to add seam allowance as all the stitching is done on the right side.

2 Pin the legs together and stitch them together along the outside edge. Start and stop at the top of the legs, leaving the base unsewn. Insert two chenille stems into each leg and then fold over the ends inside so they don't interfere with stitching the body to the legs.

3 Pin the triangular insert into the back piece and stitch it in place matching the straight edges. Pin the front and back

together; stitch up either side from the stomach around the arms all the way up to the head, leaving the head and hat unstitched.

4 Pin and then stitch the base of the body to the top of the legs.

5 Pour pellets through the opening in the head until the base is weighted.

6 Fold over an inch at either end of the fifth chenille stem. Working inside the body, thread the shaped ends inside each mitten so the center of the chenille stem spans between the arms.

7 Stuff the remainder of the body and head with fiberfill. Position a sixth chenille stem between the layers of the hat. Stitch the sides of the head and hat together.

8 Brush a generous coating of white paint over the entire finished base. Allow the paint to dry completely before continuing. Trim away the fraying edges, being careful not to cut into any of the seams with scissors.

9 *To finish the snowman,* paint the shirt and hat light blue. Use dark blue paint to paint his feet and to edge the shirt cuffs and hat brim. Add a dark blue zipper stripe up the middle of the shirt

and paint a small red heart over the upper left side of the shirt. Use the fine brush to outline the snowman's face. Fill in the carrot nose with orange paint. Let the paint dry completely. Hot-glue the wide chenille stems around the snowman's shirt collar and waist. Hot-glue the white pom-pom to the end of the hat and a light blue pom-pom to the end of each foot.

10 *To finish the Santa,* paint the Santa's shirt and hat red and his mittens and pants light green. Paint Santa's boots black and then use a fine brush and more black to outline Santa's face. Use a little pink paint to blush his cheeks and gray paint to add dimension to his beard. Wrap a wide chenille stem around Santa's neck to make his coat collar and then bring the stem end down the front of the jacket. Wrap a second stem around the base of the jacket. Hot-glue both stems in place and then wrap short chenille lengths around the top of the boots, mitten cuffs, and the base of his hat. Hot-glue the white pom-pom to the end of the hat and the small red pom-poms to the ends of the boots.

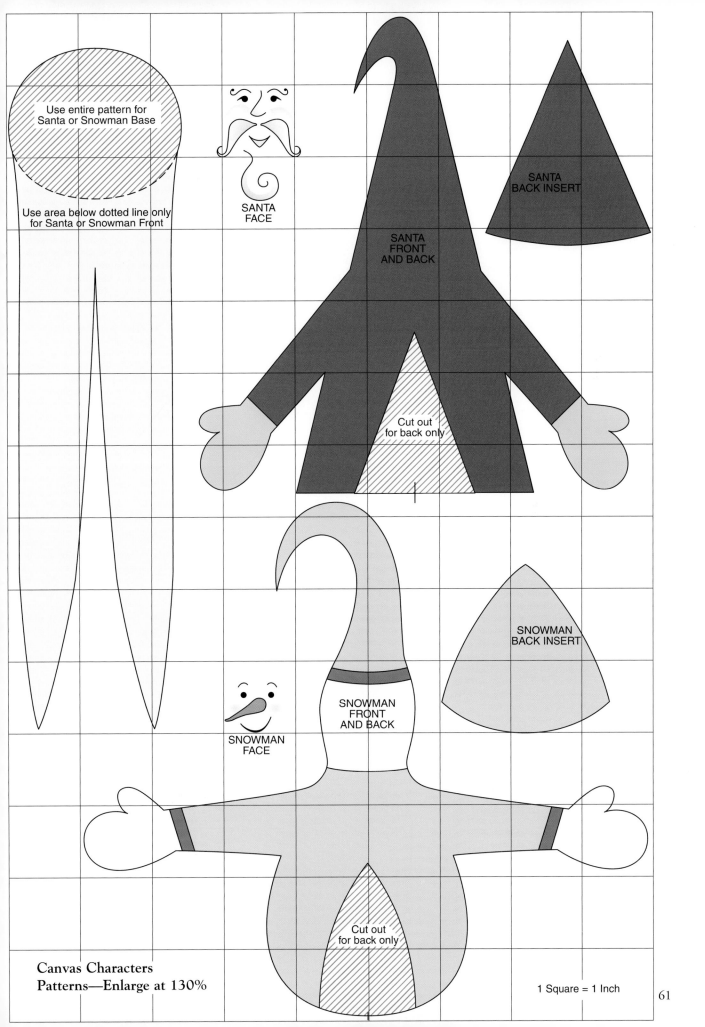

Use entire pattern for
Santa or Snowman Base

Use area below dotted line only
for Santa or Snowman Front

SANTA
FACE

SANTA
FRONT
AND BACK

SANTA
BACK INSERT

Cut out
for back only

SNOWMAN
BACK INSERT

SNOWMAN
FRONT
AND BACK

SNOWMAN
FACE

Cut out
for back only

**Canvas Characters
Patterns—Enlarge at 130%**

1 Square = 1 Inch

61

Snow Lady Sue Pillow

shown on page 53

WHAT YOU NEED

Tracing paper; pencil; scissors
20-inch square of white fleece
⅛ yard of patterned fleece
28-inch square of red fleece
Scrap of pink fleece; black thread
Straight pins; sewing machine
Five ¾-inch black buttons
Four ⅝-inch black buttons
Sewing needle; white thread
28-inch square of pink fleece
18-inch-square pillow form

HERE'S HOW

1 Enlarge and trace the pattern, *right*. Cut out each pattern piece.

2 Use the patterns to cut the snow lady, nose, and hat shapes from the fleece. Cut four small circles from white for snow. Cut two 5×11-inch strips for scarf.

3 Pin the nose on the face; zigzag-stitch the edges. Pin the snow lady to the red fleece square, centered right to left and 5 inches from the bottom edge. Zigzag the edges. Pin hat in place; zigzag edges.

4 Pin one scarf piece on the snow lady's neck, gathering at the ends. Stitch the ends to secure. Tie a knot in the center of the remaining scarf piece. Cut 2-inch-long fringes on each end. Hand-stitch the knot to the pillow top at the right end of the scarf piece.

5 Sew the button mouth and eyes in place. Zigzag eyebrows.

6 Cut a 1½×10-inch strip from solid pink fleece. Tie into a bow. Cut a notch in each end. Hand-sew the knot of the bow to the hat.

7 Sew the snow circles to the pillow top using three intersecting straight stitches; knot on back side.

8 Pin the pillow top to the pillow back. Cut 4-inch fringes around the squares through both layers.

9 Tie together three sides of the pillow fringes. Insert the pillow form. Tie the remaining fringes together. Machine-zigzag just inside the tied fringes.

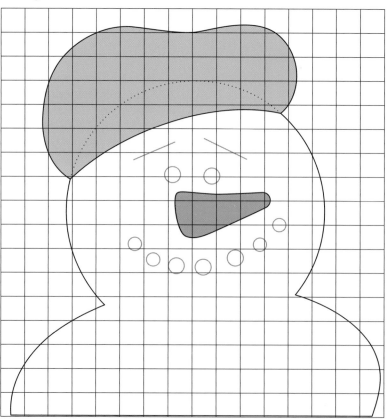

Chenille Santa Snow Gal

shown on page 54

WHAT YOU NEED

Ruler; scissors
¼ yard of off-white chenille
⅛ yard each of cotton home decorating fabric: maroon with beige stars; green with beige spots; green, beige, and blue stripes
Sewing machine; green thread
Plastic pellets; fiberfill
9-inch-long ¼-inch-wide dowel rod
3 beige chenille stems

Snow Lady Sue Pillow Patterns
Enlarge at 400%

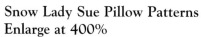

1 Square = 1 Inch

Off-white yarn or embroidery thread
2 mini pom-poms
Hot-glue gun and glue sticks
Wood ball head
Fine paintbrush
Acrylic paints in pink, orange,
    beige, and black
Moss green feathered trim
Straight pins

HERE'S HOW

1 For the base cut a 7×11-inch-long strip of chenille fabric. Cut a 4-inch-wide circle of green fabric with beige spots. Stitch a loose seam along the top edge of the chenille strip to use later to gather the fabric. Place the right sides together; machine-stitch the bottom edge of the chenille fabric around the outside edge of the green circle. Stitch the chenille sides together to shape the fabric into a tube with a circle base. Turn the fabric right side out. Pour about 2 cups of pellets into the tube base. Insert the dowel rod into the center of the pellets and fill the remainder of the base with fiberfill. Pull the thread ends at the top of the chenille to gather the fabric.

2 For the body cut a 2½×8 inch strip of maroon star fabric. Stitch a single loose seam along the top and bottom edges of the fabric strip. Fold the fabric in half and stitch the 2½-inch sides together. Turn the tube right side out and slide it down over the dowel rod. Pull the thread ends to gather the bottom seam around the dowel rod and then knot the threads. Place fiberfill around the dowel rod to stuff the base of the tube.

3 For the arms use scissors points to poke a small hole on either side of the tube body half an inch down from the top. Insert a chenille stem through a hole and then wrap the chenille end around the dowel rod. Fold the length of the chenille stem in half to shorten

MITTEN

Chenille Santa Snow Gal

Full-Size Patterns

HAT

and thicken the arm. Repeat the process to add another chenille-stem arm through the second hole. Wrap white yarn (or thread) around the folded chenille to camouflage the folded layers. Stuff the remainder of the body and then pull the thread ends to gather the top of the body closed; knot the threads. Hot-glue two mini pom-pom buttons down the center of the finished body.

4 For the head use the fine brush and paint the wood ball beige. Make a triangular carrot nose in the center of the face with orange paint. Use black paint to outline the nose and draw two circle eyes with small raised eyebrows and an upturned mouth. Blush the cheeks and highlight the center of the nose with pink paint. Let the paint dry.

5 For the hat use the pattern, *left*, as a guide to cut the hat out of the maroon star fabric. Fold the right sides of the fabric together and machine-stitch a single seam up the cut edges, leaving the bottom edge unsewn. Turn the hat right side out. Thread one end of a chenille stem into the top of the hat. Spiral the other end of the chenille stem into a 1-inch-wide circle. Hot-glue the spiraled circle onto the top of the snow gal's head. Place the seam at the back of the snow gal's head; hot-glue the bottom edge of the hat around the snow gal's face and back of her head. Trim the hat by hot-gluing a ½-inch-wide strip of chenille fabric around the base of the hat. Hot-glue a small section of green feather trim to the end of the hat to make the tassel.

6 Fill the cavity in the underside of the finished head with hot glue and then push the head down over the top of the wood dowel so it sits on top of the finished body.

7 For the scarf cut two 12-inch-long strips of green stripe fabric; pin the strips wrong sides together so that the right sides face outward. Machine-stitch the layers together making a continuous seam around all four edges. Finish the scarf by machine-stitching a section of green feather trim to the short ends of the scarf. Loosely tie the finished scarf around the snow gal's dowel-rod neck.

8 For the mittens fold the green fabric in half and use the pattern, *above left*, to cut out two pairs of mittens. Pin each pair wrong sides together (right sides out); stitch together making a continuous seam around the outside edges, leaving the bottom edge unsewn. Slide a stitched mitten onto the ends of each chenille stem arm. Cut a ¼-inch-wide strip of chenille fabric and hot-glue a section around each mitten cuff.

Smiling Snowmen

shown on pages 54–55

WHAT YOU NEED

Toothpick
Thick white crafts glue
1- and 1½-inch foam balls, such as
    Styrofoam; rolling pin
Polymer clay, such as Sculpey, in
    white, orange, and other
    desired colors
Pencil; scissors
Decorative-edge scissors
Twigs
Glass baking dish
Paintbrush; white glitter

HERE'S HOW

1 Coat one end of a toothpick with crafts glue. Push it into a 1½-inch foam ball. Coat the exposed toothpick with glue. Push it into the 1-inch ball. Let the glue dry.

2 On a flat work surface, roll out white clay until it is ⅛ inch thick. Place the clay piece over the foam balls, shaping to form. Press the bottom flat.

3 Use a sharp pencil to press in eyes, a smile, nose, and buttons. Shape a tiny carrot from orange clay and press into the nose hole.

4 Using the photos, *above* and on *page 55*, as inspiration, make clay hats and scarves as desired. To make a scarf, roll out the clay and cut the shape with scissors. Cut stripes with decorative-edge scissors and press into place. Place on the snowman.

5 Cut 2½-inch-long twigs for arms. Press a twig into each side of body. Bake

the snowmen on a glass baking dish as directed by the clay manufacturer. Let the snowmen cool.

6 Brush each snowman with water-thinned glue. Sprinkle glitter on the wet glue. Let dry.

Jolly Lollipops

shown on page 56

WHAT YOU NEED

Polymer clay in white, red, green,
    pink, light blue, and light green
Rolling pin or pasta machine
    designated for clay use
2½-inch biscuit cutter
2-inch cookie cutter or small lid
Lollipop sticks; baking sheet
Eye pins
Cellophane bags
Embroidery floss
⅛-inch-wide ribbon

HERE'S HOW

1 Knead the white and green clays separately until they are both pliable. Roll each color into a smooth ⅛-inch-thick sheet.

2 Sandwich a piece of the green sheet between two pieces of the white sheet. Press the biscuit cutter down into the stacked clay and then lift out the lollipop base. To make the decorative candy pieces, roll out coils of all the different clay colors. Stack them side by side and roll them flat or pass them

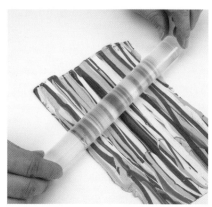

through the pasta machine. The colors should connect into a solid sheet of clay. Fold the sheet in half and press it flat again with either a rolling pin or pasta machine. Continue adding coils and flattening the sheet until satisfied with the color stripes; then press out two circles with the round cutter. Adhere a colorful circle onto the front and back of the lollipop base.

3 Push a lollipop stick up through the bottom of the clay candy. Press an eye pin down into the top of the finished lollipop. Place on a baking sheet.

4 Bake according to clay manufacturer's directions. Let cool.

5 Push an inverted cellophane bag down over the top of the lollipop. The eye pin will break through the bottom seam in the bag. Wrap a ribbon around the bunched cellophane at the base of the clay candy and tie it into a decorative bow. Thread a string of embroidery floss through the eye pin, bring the ends together, and tie them in an overhand knot for hanging.

Snow Fella Ornaments

shown on page 56

WHAT YOU NEED

Flattened round clear glass
ornaments
Paint markers, such as Uchida, in
black, green, red, orange, and
white
White glitter

HERE'S HOW

1 Place an ornament over a snowman
pattern. Draw the snowman on the
front of the ornament, outlining it
in black. Color in the design. To
prevent colors from bleeding, let each
color dry before painting the adjacent
sections.

2 Remove the ornament
cap hanger. Pour glitter
into the ornament and
replace the cap.

**Snow Fella Ornaments
Full-Size Patterns**

65

Snuggle-Up Santa Throw

shown on page 57

WHAT YOU NEED

Tracing paper
Pencil
Scissors
¼ yard of red plaid fleece
Scraps of fleece in green plaid and
    solid green, beige, and white
Scrap of faux sheepskin
Straight pins
Solid blue fleece blanket
Black thread
Sewing machine
Two ¼-inch black buttons
Three ¼-inch red buttons
Two 1-inch green buttons
One 1-inch red button

HERE'S HOW

1 Enlarge and trace the patterns, *opposite* and on *page 68*. Cut out the patterns.

2 Use the patterns to cut the shapes from fleece pieces and sheepskin.

3 Position and pin the sheepskin placket to the jacket front. Zigzag stitch the edge of each piece.

4 Position and pin the jacket onto the corner of the blanket. Zigzag-stitch.

5 Position and pin the face, beard, mustache, eyebrows, nose pom-pom, hat, brim, and snow in place. Zigzag-stitch the pieces to secure. Sew the holly onto the hat by zigzagging down the center of each leaf. Clip all threads.

6 Sew the button eyes, berries, and coat buttons in place.

Snuggle-Up Santa Throw Placement Diagram

Snuggle-Up Santa Throw Patterns
Enlarge at 200%   (continued on page 68)

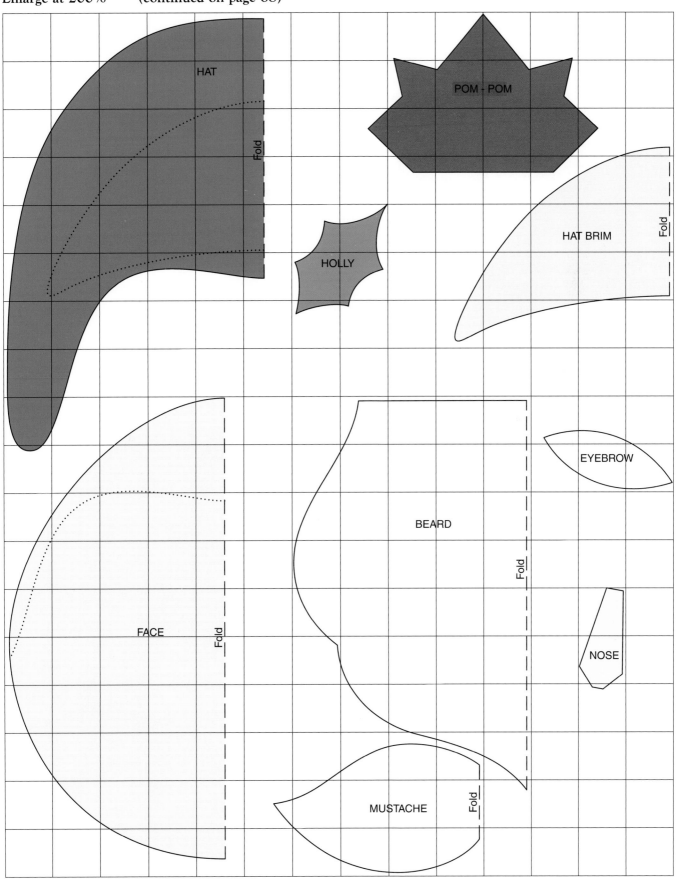

1 Square = 1 Inch

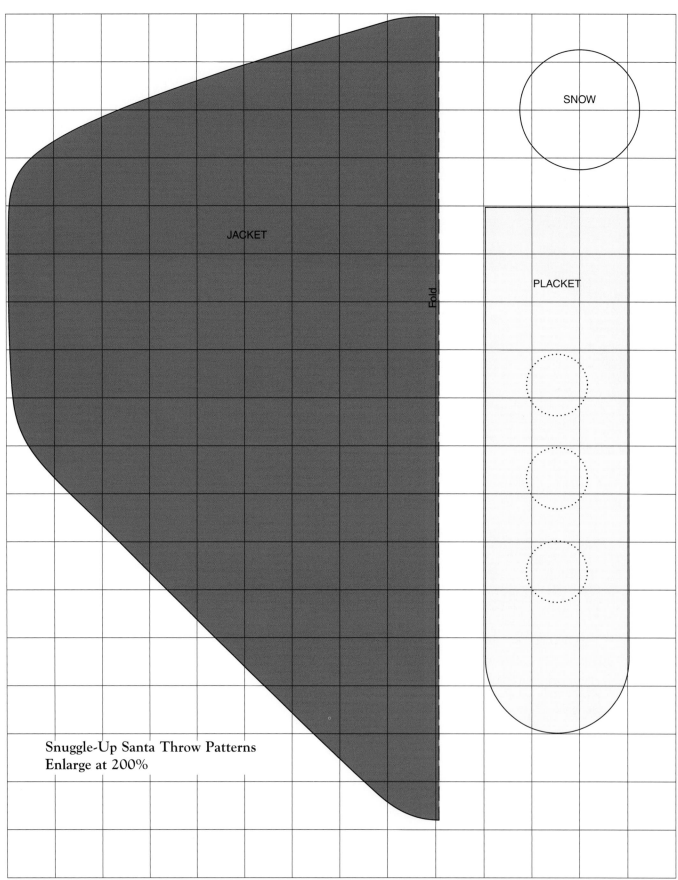

SNOW

JACKET

Fold

PLACKET

**Snuggle-Up Santa Throw Patterns
Enlarge at 200%**

1 Square = 1 Inch

Carefree Characters

shown on page 58

WHAT YOU NEED

Scissors; sock
Round white glass ornament
Hot-glue gun and glue sticks
Pom-poms in green, red, or silver
Fishing line or thread
Yarn needle; yarn
Black permanent marking pen
Pink makeup blush and brush
Wire cutters
Orange plastic-coated wire
Sharpened pencil

HERE'S HOW

1 Cut off the cuff portion of the sock, approximately 5 inches from the top. Stretch the cuff piece over the glass ornament, covering the hook. Fold back a ½-inch cuff. Hot-glue the sock in place, allowing enough room for the snowman face. To trim the hat, hot-glue pom-poms on it as desired.

2 For a hanging loop cut fishing line and tie through the loop on the ornament. Knot the ends to secure.

3 To finish cap, gather 1 or 2 inches from the top with yarn. Pull snug and knot the yarn ends. If desired, fringe the top cap piece.

4 Draw a face on the ornament with marking pen. Apply blush for cheeks.

5 For nose wrap orange wire around pencil tip, allowing the tip to gradually get smaller. Cut with wire cutters. Hot-glue nose in place.

Front Door Frosty

shown on page 59

WHAT YOU NEED

Metal snowman-shape cake pan
Newspapers
White spray primer for metal
Acrylic paints for metal in white, black, and pink
Paintbrush; artificial snow flecks
Scissors
⅛ yard of red and green plaid flannel fabric
Ruler
Thick white crafts glue
1-inch red pom-pom
Two 1-inch black buttons
Two ⅝-inch black shank buttons
Braid
4-inch-square piece of green felt
Scrap of red felt

HERE'S HOW

1 Wash and dry the cake pan. In a well-ventilated work area, cover the surface with newspapers. Spray-paint the outside of the pan with primer. Let the primer dry. Spray on a second coat of primer. Let dry.

2 Mix a small amount of white acrylic paint with artificial snow flecks. Using the photo, *above*, as a guide, paint the snowman body with the paint. Let the paint dry. Paint the details on the snowman. Let dry.

3 Cut the two strips of fabric, each approximately 4×3 inches. Fold and shape the fabric into a scarf and glue it in place. Glue the pom-pom, buttons, and braid on the snowman.

4 From the green felt cut two holly leaf shapes. Cut three circles from red felt for berries. Glue the felt pieces on the hat. Let dry.

paper
treasures

Combine your creativity with lovely papers to make cards that will shower family and friends with handmade greetings.

Familiar Christmas symbols can be duplicated on paper using a variety of crafty techniques. The **Jolly Holly Card**, *opposite*, is a colorful cutout and layered paper design. Hold pleats in place with machine stitches to make **Elegant Evergreens** topped with a gold hand-stitched star. Instructions and patterns are on *pages 78–79*.

Dozens of cards are waiting to be assembled from your

collection of fabric, paper, and ribbon scraps. With just the

right details, your handmade greetings are ready to send. The

Vintage Stocking Card mixes a pretty calico with soft chenille

for a classic Victorian look. For a contemporary feel craft a

Snow Sisters Card, *opposite*, that incorporates wire and

stamping into the design. Instructions and patterns are on

pages 79–80.

These holiday cards are so clever, they're sure to be saved as precious heirlooms. The **Prints Charming** card, *opposite*, showcases family photos in tiny gold charms. As a tribute to St. Nick, create **Ho Ho Ho Hello** cards that feel as feathery as they look. For a bright design use paper scraps in a multitude of colors to deliver warmth in **Merry Mittens Note Cards.** Instructions and patterns are on *pages 80–82*.

Dimensional embellishments are the main attractions on these classy Christmas cards. For **Simply Charming** cards, coordinating paper punches and a single charm offer hints of magic. The **Beaded Wreath Greetings,** *opposite*, are sparkling sensations with rings of beads and metallic sequins set on silver paper. Instructions are on *page 83*.

paper treasures

Jolly Holly Card

shown on page 70

WHAT YOU NEED

Tracing paper; pencil; scissors
Vellum sheets in white and
 2 shades of green; ruler
4¼×5½-inch purchased white
 vellum card envelope; crafts knife
Scrap of red dot vellum sheet
Circle holiday greeting stamp

Red stamp pad, such as Brilliance,
 that works well on vellum paper
Aleene's 2 and 1 glue

HERE'S HOW

1 Trace the patterns, *below left*, onto tracing paper. Cut out the shapes.
2 Fold the white vellum in half. Trim to make a 4¼×5½-inch card. Open the card and trace around the pattern on the card front.
3 Working over a protected surface, use a crafts knife to cut the larger leaf pattern out of the front of the card.
4 Fold one of the green vellum sheets in half and trim it to 4¼×5½ inches; slide it into the white card to show through the cutout hole in the first step; glue in place.
5 Stamp the round message onto the white vellum below the cut-out leaf. While the stamped message dries, cut the smaller leaf pattern out of the second shade of green vellum and the partial berry out of red dotted vellum.
6 Glue the second leaf alongside the first cut-out leaf. Glue the dotted partial berry alongside the stamped message to give the appearance of two holly berries. Let dry.

Elegant Evergreens

shown on page 71

WHAT YOU NEED

6½×10-inch piece of red card stock
4½×6-inch piece of contrasting
 paper, such as green or gold
Pinking shears
Sewing machine and thread

Tracing paper; pencil; scissors
5½×6½-inch piece of coordinating
 print scrapbook paper for tree
Tapestry needle
Metallic gold decorative thread

HERE'S HOW

1 Fold the red card stock in half, short ends together.
2 Trim the edge of the contrasting paper rectangle using pinking shears. Center the contrasting paper rectangle on the card front. Machine-stitch in place leaving a narrow border.
3 Trace the tree pattern, *opposite*. Use the pattern and straight scissors or pinking shears to cut a tree from scrapbook paper. Cut a ½×2½-inch tree trunk.
4 Use the diagrams, *below*, to pleat the paper triangle. Stitch the edge of each pleat to secure. Arrange the tree and trunk papers on the card front and machine-stitch in place, sewing vertically down the center.
5 To stitch the star topper, use the needle to poke six holes at the tip of the paper tree, one at the center with five holes evenly spaced around it.
6 Thread the needle with gold decorative thread. Sew long straight stitching between opposite holes. End on the card back; knot the ribbon ends.

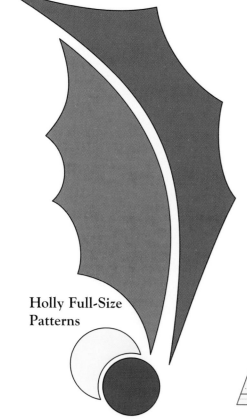

Holly Full-Size Patterns

Elegant Evergreens Folding Diagrams

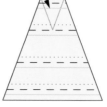 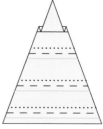 

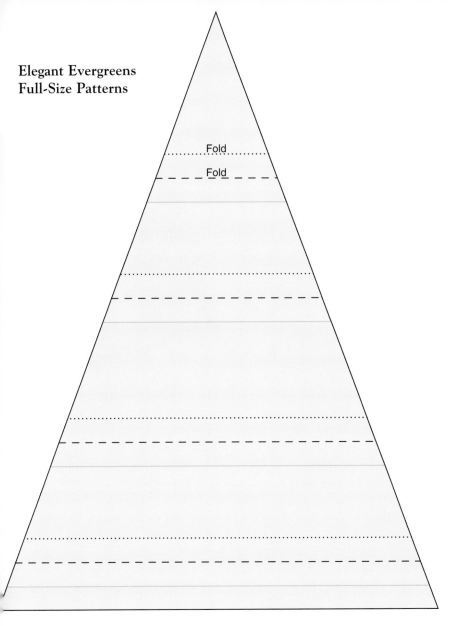

**Elegant Evergreens
Full-Size Patterns**

Fold

Fold

2 Follow the package instructions to iron the fusible web to the underside of the calico scrap. Trace the patterns, *below;* cut out. Use pattern to cut the stocking out of the prepared calico and the cuff out of the chenille.

3 Apply toy stickers to the blue rectangle, overlapping them to give the appearance that they are tucked into the stocking.

4 Position the calico stocking below the stickers leaving a blank space that later will be covered with the chenille cuff. Open the card and machine-stitch around the stocking edge to attach it to the card. (Note: It's a good idea to test the stitching with fabric and paper scraps first before sewing on the card.)

5 Glue the chenille along the top edge of the calico stocking. Tie the ribbon in a decorative bow and glue it to the left side of the stocking cuff. Let dry.

**Vintage Stocking Card
Full-Size Patterns**

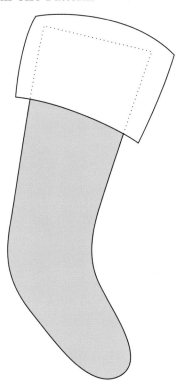

Vintage Stocking Card

shown on page 72

WHAT YOU NEED

Ivory card stock
Ruler
Glue stick
Gold pattern scrapbook paper
Thick white crafts glue
Blue card stock
Iron; fusible web
Tracing paper; pencil
Calico cotton fabric scrap
Chenille scrap; scissors
Toy stickers
Sewing machine
Green thread
⅛-inch-wide ivory satin ribbon
4⅜×5¾-inch ivory envelope

HERE'S HOW

1 Fold the ivory card stock in half; trim it to make a card 4¼×5½ inches. Trim the gold paper to measure 3⅜×4¾ inches. Glue it in the center of the card. Trim blue card stock to 3⅛×4½ inches and glue it in the center of the gold paper.

Snow Sisters Card

shown on page 73

WHAT YOU NEED

Textured white paper

¹⁄₁₆-inch hole punch

Scissors

Tracing paper; pencil

Card stock in light blue, red,
   orange, and dark blue

Thick white crafts glue

Sewing needle

26-gauge silver wire

Snowflake stamp

Stamp pad in white or silver

6-inch square silver square
   envelope

HERE'S HOW

1 From textured white paper tear or
cut two nickel-size circles for the

Snow Sisters Card
Full-Size Patterns

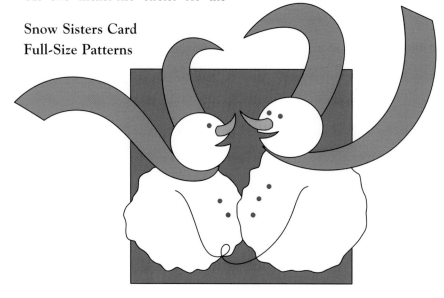

snowmen's heads and two quarter-size
circles for their bodies.

2 Punch eyeholes using the pattern as
a guide. Use scissors to cut out a small
smiling mouth on each snowman.
Punch button holes down the bodies.

3 Cut a 2¼×2⅜-inch square of dark
blue card stock.

4 Glue the snowmen pieces side by
side on the blue square so they appear to
be facing each other. Trace the scarf and
carrot nose patterns, *below*. Use patterns
to cut out shapes from red and silver
card stock. Glue these pieces onto the
snowmen, allowing scarves to extend
beyond the edges of the blue square.

5 Use a needle to poke an armhole
through each snowman's shoulders.
Make a loop in the center of a 4-inch
wire length and then thread each end of
the wire through a prepared shoulder
hole. Fold the wire ends flat behind the
blue square.

6 Fold the light blue card stock in half
and trim it to make a 5½-inch-square
card. Mount the blue square to the
center of the light blue card.

7 Stamp snowflakes around the
snowmen. Let dry.

Prints Charming

shown on page 74

WHAT YOU NEED

Favorite family photographs

Color photocopier, optional

Scissors

Thick white crafts glue

Mini frames, such as Nunn Design

Small paintbrush

Paper glaze

Solid card stock in black, red,
   and gold

Holiday print card stock in green
   and red

Ruler; tracing paper; pencil

Double-sided tape

Gold mini brads

Single-sided tape

HERE'S HOW

1 If necessary, make reduced size color
copies of the photos or use original
pictures small enough to fit inside the
hang tags. Cut out the images to fit
inside the tags.

2 Glue the images into the hang tag
frames. Let dry. Brush the photo images
in the tags with two coats of paper glaze,
allowing drying time between coats.

3 Cut the black card stock to measure
10×15 inches. Fold it in half to make

Prints Charming Full-Size Patterns

Ho Ho Ho Hello

shown in page 75

WHAT YOU NEED
- Red paper
- Scissors; ruler
- White cardstock
- Glue stick
- Black felt tip marking pen
- Lower case stamp alphabet
- Black stamp pad
- Tracing paper
- Pencil
- Plaid print scrapbook paper
- Standard hole punch
- Metallic green paper
- Thick white crafts glue
- White feathers
- Red business-size envelope

HERE'S HOW

1 Fold the red paper in half lengthwise with the short ends together; trim it to make a 9×3½-inch card.

2 Trim the white card stock sheet to measure 8½×3 inches. Use a glue stick to mount it to the center of the red card.

3 Use the black marking pen to draw Santa's eyes, eyebrows, and nose a third of the way down from the top of the card. Use the letter "o" stamp to add a round mouth below Santa's nose. Onto the lower third of the card, stamp the message "ho ho ho" using both the "h" and "o" stamps.

4 Trace the hat pattern, *below*. Use the pattern to cut out Santa's plaid hat and glue it above his face. Punch a metallic green pom-pom and glue it to the top of the hat.

5 Use crafts glue to attach a white feather beard below Santa's mouth, a small feather mustache above his mouth, and a feather trim along the bottom edge of the hat. Let dry.

Ho Ho Ho Hello
Full-Size Patterns

the card. Cut the green holiday paper to measure 4×6½ inches. Trace the patterns, *above*, and cut out. Use the patterns to cut the remaining shapes as shown in the photo, *opposite*. Use double-sided tape to adhere the tree, trunk, and base to the green holiday paper. Tape the two star shapes together and adhere to green paper.

4 Position the charms on the tree. Mark their positions at the charm loops. Very gently pierce a small point at each pencil mark. Thread a brad through each charm loop and through the layers of paper. Spread brad ends and tape them down with single-sided tape. Adhere the green holiday paper with tree to the black card using double-sided tape.

mitten shape from card stock in a contrasting color.

3 Cut various-width strips from color paper and card stock. Glue horizontally on mitten shape, layering strips where desired. Trim strips even with the edge of the mitten.

4 Punch seven holes ¼ inch apart along cuff section of mitten shape. Cut fourteen 6-inch lengths of yarn. Fold yarn pieces in half two at a time. Insert the yarn folds into one hole in the mitten from the back. Thread the ends through the loop and pull snugly. Repeat for each hole. Trim yarn ends slightly beyond the edge of the card. Embellish the tip of the envelope flap in the same manner if desired.

5 Glue the mitten shape in the center of the card front.

Merry Mittens Note Cards

shown on page 75

WHAT YOU NEED

8½×5¼-inch rectangle of white
  card stock
Glue stick
4×5-inch rectangle of color card
  stock for background
Tracing paper; pencil
Scissors
4×5-inch rectangle of contrasting
  card stock for mitten
Scraps of paper and card stock in
  desired colors
Paper punch; ruler
Variegated yarn
Envelope

HERE'S HOW

1 Fold the white card stock in half, short ends together. Using glue stick, adhere the color paper rectangle to the front of the card.

2 Trace the mitten pattern, *right,* and cut it out. Use the pattern to cut a

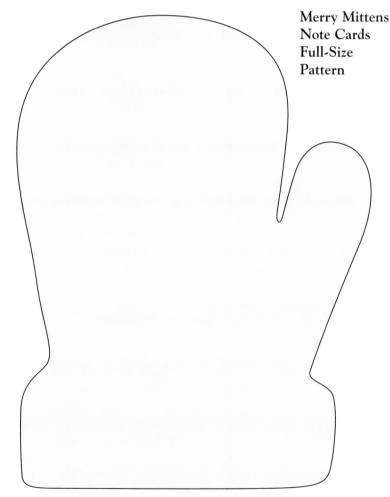

**Merry Mittens
Note Cards
Full-Size
Pattern**

ribbon with the prepared silver paper, making sure the metallic side appears through the punched openings.

4 Close the cover and begin tying the ribbon ends into a bow. Stop midway to thread a silver charm onto one ribbon end before finishing the bow. Trim the ribbon ends and place small pieces of double-sided tape under the ribbon to help secure the bow flat against the greeting card.

5 Center the stamped season's greeting message below the punched stars.

Simply Charming

shown on page 76

WHAT YOU NEED

Card stock in light blue or pink

Ruler

Paper cutter or scissors

Silver metallic paper

2 sizes of star or heart paper punches

Thick white crafts glue

1 yard of ½-inch-wide organza ribbon

Silver charm

Double-sided tape

Season's greetings stamp and silver stamp pad

White square envelopes

HERE'S HOW

1 Fold the card stock in half and trim it to make a 5½-inch square. Trim the silver metallic paper to the same size as the card so that it fits perfectly inside the card; set it aside.

2 Working on the front of the card, punch a random strip of small- and medium-size stars or hearts ½ inch up from the bottom edge.

3 Working inside the card, apply glue to the underside of the front cover. Position the center of the ribbon length in the glue 1 to 2 inches from the top of the card. Cover both the glue and

Beaded Wreath Greetings

shown on page 77

WHAT YOU NEED

Silver plus coordinating color blue, red or green seed beads

10-inch length of 26-gauge wire

Shaped sequins

Needle-nose pliers

Colored card stock

Coordinating card stock

Scissors

Metallic silver paper

Crafts knife

8-inch length ⅛-inch-wide satin ribbon

Silver letter stickers

HERE'S HOW

1 Randomly string 8 inches of seed beads onto the 10-inch wire length (if necessary tape one end so the beads don't fall off while working).

2 Coil the beaded wire into a double circle wreath. Twist one of the wire ends around the two thicknesses of beaded wire to hold them together.

3 To give the wreath a focal point, thread a combination of large to small shaped sequins onto each wire end. To finish, thread a single bead onto each wire end and use needle-nose pliers to bend over the wire end to prevent the beads and sequins from falling off.

4 Fold the colored card stock in half and trim it to make a 4×5½-inch card. Cut a coordinating 2¼×2½-inch square of card stock and mount it to one side of the card. Cut a 2-inch square of metallic silver paper and mount it to the center of the coordinating card stock square.

5 Open the card and place it on a protected surface. Use a crafts knife to cut two horizontal ¼-inch-long slits ¼ inch apart at the center top of the silver square. From inside the card push the ribbon ends through the slits and then pull them out the front of the card. Position the top of the beaded wreath between the ribbon ends and tie them together in a bow.

6 Mount the silver letter stickers alongside the mounted wreath to spell a simple holiday message such as "Peace" or "Joy."

gifts from the kitchen

Head into the kitchen (instead of out to the mall) to create memorable gifts you'll be proud to share.

Decadent Hot Chocolate Mix, *opposite*, makes the richest, dreamiest hot chocolate around. Present alongside the cute candy-dipped marshmallows for a merry treat indeed. Families also will enjoy a bag brimming with **Popcorn and Candy Balls**, *below*, especially when you call on holiday-hued candies that add to the colorful presentation. The recipes are on *page 92*.

Mixes make great gifts! Recipients can savor them at their convenience after the holidays are over. **Cranberry-Apple Granola Muffin Mix,** *left*, will make a weekend morning breakfast special. Friends who receive a bag of **Ultimate Chili Mix,** *below*, will be especially grateful when the cold January wind blows. **Tropical Cookie Drops Mix,** *opposite*, also will brighten the winter days ahead. The recipes are on *pages 92–93*.

Tropical Coconut Drops

Empty contents of jar into a large bowl, stir until mixed. In small bowl combine 1 slightly beaten egg 2 tbsp. pineapple juice or milk and ½ tsp. vanilla, add to flour mixture in bowl. Stir until combined. Drop dough by rounded teaspoons 2 inches apart onto ungreased cookie sheets. Bake in a 375 F oven for 9–10 minutes or just until lightly browned. Transfer to wire racks, cool.

Stop by a friend's house with one of these goodies, then stay a while to share them over a nice long chat—that's what the holidays are all about. **Cherry-Pecan Bread,** *opposite*, freezes beautifully. Just thaw and glaze before serving. As easy as a quick bread, yet as moist and luscious as a cake, **Orange-Poppy Seed Loaf Cake**, *below*, is a treat anyone will cherish. Offer either with a tin of gourmet tea or a bag of coffee from your favorite local coffeehouse. The recipes are on *page 94*.

Sweet Cheese Tortes, *below,* make for a luscious bite at tea-time. You know how elegant truffles are! Now see how easy they are to make. In just a few quick, easy steps, **Spiced Brandy Truffles,** *center,* can be set to dazzle. **Pretzel Yummies,** *opposite,* could easily become your signature holiday confection, for there's nothing quite like them! The recipes are on *pages 94–95*.

Decadent Hot Chocolate Mix

shown on page 84

WHAT YOU NEED

1	cup sugar
1	cup unsweetened cocoa powder
2	cups nonfat dry milk powder
1½	cups large or regular semisweet chocolate pieces
1	cup coarsely chopped soft peppermint sticks
1½	cups large or regular milk chocolate pieces

HERE'S HOW

1 In three 1-pint glass jars, layer sugar, cocoa powder, milk powder, semisweet chocolate, chopped peppermint sticks, and milk chocolate, dividing equally. Seal; attach directions for Decadent Hot Chocolate. Store in a cool, dry place up to 1 month. Makes 3 jars (4 servings each).

To Make Decadent Hot Chocolate: In a saucepan combine contents of jar with 1⅔ cups water. Heat and stir over medium heat until hot and chocolate pieces melt. Pour into 4 mugs. Serve with Double-Dipped Marshmallows.

Double-Dipped Marshmallows: In a small saucepan heat 8 ounces chopped semisweet chocolate baking squares and 2 teaspoons shortening over low heat until melted, stirring constantly. Remove from heat. Using your fingers, carefully dip half of each of 24 large marshmallows into the melted chocolate, letting excess drip off. Immediately sprinkle each with crushed candy canes (about ½ cup). Place on waxed paper until chocolate is set. Wrap in clear plastic wrap; tie with ribbons.

Popcorn and Candy Balls

shown on page 85

WHAT YOU NEED

20	cups popped popcorn
1½	cups light-colored corn syrup
1½	cups sugar
1	7-ounce jar marshmallow creme
2	tablespoons butter
1	teaspoon vanilla
1½	cups candy-coated milk chocolate pieces or candy-coated peanut butter-flavored pieces

HERE'S HOW

1 Remove all unpopped kernels from popped popcorn. Place popcorn in a buttered 17×12×2-inch baking pan or roasting pan. Keep the popcorn warm in a 300°F oven while preparing marshmallow mixture.

2 In a large saucepan bring corn syrup and sugar to boiling over medium-high heat, stirring constantly. Remove from heat. Stir in marshmallow creme, butter, and vanilla until combined.

3 Pour marshmallow mixture over hot popcorn; stir gently to coat. Cool until popcorn mixture can be handled easily. Stir in candies. With damp hands quickly shape mixture into 3-inch-diameter balls. Wrap each popcorn ball in plastic wrap. Store at room temperature up to 1 week. Makes 24 popcorn balls.

Cranberry-Apple Granola Muffin Mix

shown on page 86

WHAT YOU NEED

1	cup all-purpose flour
2	teaspoons baking powder
¼	teaspoon baking soda
¾	cup whole wheat flour
½	teaspoon ground cinnamon
⅛	teaspoon ground allspice
½	cup packed brown sugar
¾	cup snipped dried apples
¾	cup granola
¾	cup dried cranberries

HERE'S HOW

1 In small bowl stir together the all-purpose flour, baking powder, baking soda, and ¼ teaspoon salt. In another small bowl stir together the whole wheat flour, cinnamon, and allspice.

2 In a 1-quart glass jar, layer the whole wheat flour mixture, all-purpose flour mixture, brown sugar, apples, granola, and cranberries. Tap jar gently on the counter to settle each layer before adding the next one. Seal and attach directions for making Cranberry-Apple Granola Muffins. Store in a cool, dry place up to 1 month. Makes 1 jar (enough mix to make 18 muffins).

To Make Cranberry-Apple Granola Muffins: Grease eighteen 2½-inch muffin cups; set aside. In a large bowl whisk together 1 cup milk, 1 egg, and ¼ cup butter, melted. Add contents of jar and stir just until combined. Spoon batter into prepared muffin cups. Bake in a 400°F oven for 15 to 18 minutes or until a toothpick inserted in the centers comes out clean. Cool in muffin cups on

gifts from the kitchen

a wire rack for 5 minutes. Remove from muffin cups; serve warm.

HERE'S HOW TO MAKE GIFT JAR:

1 Gather a 26-inch-long strip of ¼-inch-wide red satin ribbon, three jingle bells, and a paper scroll containing recipe directions. String ribbon through the first bell to make longest loop (5½ inches after looped), secure top of loop with hot glue, leaving a 5-inch tail. Continue doing the same for the other two bells (approximately 4 inches and 3 inches in length). When finished, tie tails around the paper scroll. Hot-glue the ribbon to the top of the cookie jar.

Ultimate Chili Mix

shown on page 86

WHAT YOU NEED

½	cup dried minced onion
½	cup chili powder
½	cup instant espresso powder
½	cup packed brown sugar
2	tablespoons dried oregano, crushed
2	tablespoons ground cumin
4	teaspoons garlic salt
½	teaspoon ground cinnamon
½	teaspoon cayenne pepper

HERE'S HOW

1 Stir together the onion, chili powder, espresso powder, brown sugar, oregano, cumin, garlic salt, cinnamon, and cayenne pepper. Divide between four small plastic bags. Seal; attach directions for making Ultimate Chili. Store in a cool, dry place for up to 3 months. Makes 4 batches of mix, 6 servings each.

To Make Ultimate Chili: In a 4-quart Dutch oven or pot cook 1 pound lean ground beef until brown. Drain fat. Stir in two 15-ounce cans pinto beans and/or black beans, rinsed and drained; one 28-ounce can undrained crushed tomatoes; one 14-ounce can beef broth; and one bag of the chili mix. Bring to boiling; reduce heat. Cover; simmer 30 minutes, stirring occasionally. Serve with shredded cheese and sour cream, if desired.

Tropical Cookie Drops Mix

For a clever gift presentation, use a color copier to enlarge the snowman, right. Then print instructions on it and attach to the jar with decorative wire. Shown on page 87.

WHAT YOU NEED

1⅓	cups all-purpose flour
1	teaspoon baking powder
¼	teaspoon baking soda
¼	teaspoon ground ginger
¼	teaspoon salt
½	cup butter-flavored shortening
⅓	cup packed brown sugar
⅓	cup granulated sugar
¾	cup tropical-blend mixed dried fruit bits
½	cup coconut
½	cup coarsely chopped macadamia nuts or almonds

HERE'S HOW

1 Stir together flour, baking powder, baking soda, ginger, and salt. Using a pastry blender, cut in shortening until mixture resembles coarse crumbs.

2 In a 1-quart glass jar, layer in the following order: flour mixture, brown sugar, granulated sugar, fruit bits, coconut, and nuts. Tap jar gently on counter to settle each layer before adding the next one. Seal and attach directions for making Tropical Cookie Drops. Store in a cool, dry place up to 1 month. Makes 1 jar (enough for 2½ dozen cookies).

To Make Tropical Cookie Drops: Empty the contents of the jar into a large bowl; stir until mixed. In a small bowl combine 1 slightly beaten egg, 2 tablespoons pineapple juice or milk, and ½ teaspoon vanilla; add to flour mixture in bowl. Stir until combined. Drop dough by rounded teaspoons 2 inches apart onto an ungreased cookie sheet. Bake in a 375°F oven for 9 to 10 minutes or just until lightly browned. Transfer to a wire rack and let cool.

Enlarge at 200%

Cherry-Pecan Bread

shown on page 88

WHAT YOU NEED

	Nonstick cooking spray
1	10-ounce jar maraschino cherries
¼	cup all-purpose flour
½	cup chopped pecans
½	cup flaked coconut
1	8-ounce package cream cheese, softened
¾	cup butter, softened
2	cups granulated sugar
4	eggs
1¾	cups all-purpose flour
1½	teaspoons baking powder
1½	teaspoons vanilla
1	cup powdered sugar

HERE'S HOW

1 Lightly coat two 8×4×2-inch loaf pans with nonstick cooking spray. Set aside. Drain the maraschino cherries, reserving 2 tablespoons juice. Chop the cherries (should yield about ¾ cup chopped cherries). In a bowl combine the chopped cherries, the ¼ cup flour, the pecans, and coconut; set aside.

2 In a large mixing bowl beat cream cheese and butter with an electric mixer on medium speed until smooth. Gradually add granulated sugar, beating until light and fluffy. Add eggs one at a time, beating well after each addition. In a small bowl stir together the 1¾ cups flour and the baking powder. Gradually add flour mixture to cream cheese mixture. Beat in vanilla. Fold in maraschino cherry mixture. Spread batter into prepared pans.

3 Bake in a 325°F oven about 1 hour or until a toothpick inserted near centers comes out clean. Cool in pans on wire racks for 10 minutes. Remove from pans. Cool on wire racks. For easier slicing, wrap and store overnight.

4 Stir together powdered sugar and enough reserved cherry juice (4 to 6 teaspoons)* to make a glaze. Spread over bread. Makes 2 loaves (28 servings).

***Test Kitchen Tip:** If you prefer a vanilla glaze, substitute 3 to 5 teaspoons water and 1 teaspoon vanilla for the maraschino cherry juice.

Orange-Poppy Seed Loaf Cake

shown on page 89

WHAT YOU NEED

3	cups all-purpose flour
2½	cups sugar
1½	teaspoons baking powder
1½	cups milk
1	cup cooking oil
3	eggs
2	tablespoons poppy seeds
1½	teaspoons vanilla
1½	teaspoons almond extract
1½	teaspoons finely shredded orange peel (divided use)
½	cup sugar
3	tablespoons orange juice
¼	teaspoon vanilla
¼	teaspoon almond extract

HERE'S HOW

1 Grease and lightly flour the bottom and ½ inch up sides of two 8×4×2-inch loaf pans. Set aside. In a very large bowl stir together flour, the 2½ cups sugar, the baking powder, and 1 teaspoon salt.

2 Add the milk, oil, eggs, poppy seeds, the 1½ teaspoons vanilla, the 1½ teaspoons almond extract, and 1 teaspoon of the orange peel. Beat with an electric mixer on medium speed until combined. Pour into the prepared pans.

2 Bake in a 325°F oven for 65 to 70 minutes or until a toothpick inserted near the centers of loaves comes out clean. Cool in the pans on wire racks for 10 minutes.

3 Meanwhile, for glaze, in a small saucepan combine the remaining ½ teaspoon orange peel, the ½ cup sugar, the orange juice, the ¼ teaspoon vanilla, and the ¼ teaspoon almond extract. Cook and stir until the sugar is dissolved.

4 Using a long-tine fork, pierce tops of cakes all over. Slowly spoon the glaze over the warm cakes in the pans. Cool in the pans for 30 minutes more. Remove from pans; cool on wire racks. Makes 2 loaf cakes (10 servings each).

Sweet Cheese Tortes

shown on page 90

WHAT YOU NEED

½	of an 8-ounce tub cream cheese with pineapple
¼	cup butter, softened
3	tablespoons powdered sugar
½	teaspoon ground cinnamon
¼	cup finely shredded carrot
1	tablespoon finely chopped crystallized ginger
1	10¾-ounce frozen loaf pound cake, thawed

3   tablespoons apricot preserves
    Chopped crystallized ginger
    (optional)

HERE'S HOW

1 In a medium mixing bowl combine cream cheese, butter, powdered sugar, and cinnamon. Beat with an electric mixer on medium speed about 30 seconds or until combined. Stir in the carrot and the 1 tablespoon crystallized ginger.

2 Trim the crust from the thawed cake. Cut the cake in half crosswise; cut each half horizontally into thirds. Spread the cream cheese mixture over 3 of the 6 slices of cake. Place remaining cake slices on top. Cover and chill for 3 to 24 hours.

3 Cut up any large pieces of preserves. In a small saucepan melt preserves over low heat, stirring constantly. Uncover the 3 tortes and brush the tops of each with some of the apricot preserves. Place each torte on a small serving plate. Cut each torte in half, then cut in half again forming 4 squares. Cut each square in half diagonally, forming 8 small triangles per torte. If desired, top each torte triangle with chopped crystallized ginger. Store in an airtight container in the refrigerator up to 24 hours. Makes 3 tortes.

Spiced Brandy Truffles

shown on pages 90-91

WHAT YOU NEED

1   11½-ounce package milk
     chocolate pieces
½   cup chopped walnuts, toasted

¼   cup dairy sour cream
2   teaspoons brandy or
     ¼ teaspoon brandy extract
½   teaspoon ground nutmeg
     (divided use)
¼   cup powdered sugar
¼   teaspoon ground cinnamon

HERE'S HOW

1 In a small heavy saucepan, melt chocolate pieces over low heat, stirring constantly. Remove from heat. Stir in walnuts, sour cream, brandy or brandy extract, and ¼ teaspoon of the ground nutmeg. Transfer mixture to a bowl. Cover and chill at least 2 hours or until chocolate mixture is firm enough to shape into balls.

2 Line a baking sheet with waxed paper; set aside. In a small bowl combine powdered sugar, cinnamon, and the remaining ¼ teaspoon ground nutmeg. Shape chocolate mixture into ¾-inch balls. Roll each ball in the powdered sugar mixture and place on prepared baking sheet. Cover and chill until firm. Store truffles in an airtight container in the refrigerator up to 2 weeks. Let stand at room temperature about 30 minutes before serving. Makes about 30 truffles.

Pretzel Yummies

shown on page 91

WHAT YOU NEED

2   cups walnuts (8 ounces)
1   cup peanut butter-flavored
     pieces
1   cup milk chocolate pieces

1   cup packed brown sugar
½   cup light-colored corn syrup
¼   cup butter
⅔   cup sweetened condensed
     milk
½   teaspoon vanilla
25   pretzel rods or one 14-ounce
     package whole Bavarian
     pretzels

HERE'S HOW

1 In a food processor combine walnuts, peanut butter pieces, and chocolate pieces. Cover and process until mixture is coarsely chopped (or coarsely chop nuts, peanut butter pieces, and chocolate pieces with a knife and combine). Transfer mixture to a large bowl; set aside.

2 In a small heavy saucepan, combine brown sugar, corn syrup, and butter. Bring to boiling over medium heat, stirring constantly. Stir in sweetened condensed milk. Return to boiling over medium heat, stirring constantly. Reduce heat to medium-low. Clip a candy thermometer to side of pan. Continue cooking, stirring constantly, until mixture reaches 236°F, soft-ball stage (about 10 minutes). (Adjust heat as necessary to maintain a steady boil.) Remove saucepan from heat; stir in vanilla. Cool for 15 to 20 minutes or until slightly thickened.

3 Dip each pretzel into caramel mixture, covering about two-thirds of the pretzel. Let caramel drip off slightly. Spoon or roll some of the crumb mixture onto the caramel on the pretzel, pressing crumbs lightly into caramel with back of a spoon. Place on nonstick foil; let stand until caramel is set. Store in an airtight container between layers of waxed paper in refrigerator up to 4 days, or freeze up to 1 month. Makes 25 pretzel rods or 15 whole Bavarian pretzels.

decorate
the tree

*Real or artificial, flocked or natural, your
tree can reflect your favorite motifs,
from the first branch to the star at the top.*

For a bold and retro interpretation, use shapes and colors that
contrast with the texture and color of the tree. For **Festive 45s**
flavor, resurrect your collection of 45 records and hang them
proudly from dangling ribbons. Fill in the branches with **Jingle
Jangle Garlands** made from scrapbooking tags and bring music
to your holidays at every glance. Instructions are on *page 108*.

Small accents, executed with imagination, transform ordinary holiday spheres into ornaments that will make your tree branches shine. Coat an ornament with tiny tissue paper squares for **Tissued Treasures** that express colorful graphics. The **Bead-Berry Ornaments,** *opposite*, appear as though they have colorful dewdrops gracing the surface. Instructions are on *pages 108–109*.

Whether cut, folded, creased, or wrapped, scrapbook papers add artistic touches to the Christmas tree. Use the papers to wrap **Miniature Packages,** then stack and tie with a ribbon bow. To make decorative containers, fold **Star Cornucopias** to fill with tinsel and tiny holiday ornaments. Instructions and patterns are on *pages 109–110*.

Nostalgic trims are naturally sentimental and are twice as nice when handcrafted. Use old photos or make black and white copies of current snapshots to make framed **Vintage Images,** *opposite*. Super easy and incredibly pretty are **Ribbon-Wrapped Glass Ornaments,** that you'll want to make for family and friends. Instructions are on *page 111*.

Try something a little out of the ordinary on your tree this season. Add vibrant fabric-store trims to etched balls for **Sew-Merry Tree Trims**. For a touch of whimsy and a delightful twist on a naturally woodsy find, paint **Polka-Dot Mushrooms,** *opposite*. Instructions are on *page 112*.

Deck the tree in contemporary ornaments and garlands.

Cleverly Colored Ornaments, *opposite*, use an unusual paint process that will have everyone wondering how you created the colorful spheres. Readily available scrapbooking supplies hold the key to making a **Graphic Garland** with bold, gold-edge circles and squares. Instructions are on *page 113*.

Festive 45s

shown on page 96

WHAT YOU NEED
Ruler; scissors
Desired ribbon
45-style records with red, green,
    white, and silver labels

HERE'S HOW
1 For each record cut a 24-inch length of ribbon.
2 Thread the ribbon through the hole in the center of the record. Tie the ribbon ends into a bow, allowing space between the record and the bow for hanging.
3 Trim the ribbon ends if desired.

Jingle Jangle Garland

shown on pages 96–97

WHAT YOU NEED
Paintbrush
All-purpose sealer

Black-rim tags, such as Paper
    Reflections (available in
    scrapbooking stores)
Opaque red acrylic paint
Alphabet stickers, such as
    Nostalgiques Dictionary
    ABC Stickers
Matte finish spray
Silver eyelets
Eyelet setter and hammer
Silver 8 mm jump rings
Silver 15 mm jingle bells
Long-nose pliers
Scissors
Black 3mm ribbon
Ruler
White and silver garland
Silver brads
Round-nose pliers

HERE'S HOW
1 Brush the sealer onto the black-rim tags. Let the sealer dry. Brush the red paint onto the white portions of the tags. Let dry. Paint the back of the tags if desired; let dry.
2 Apply the alphabet stickers to the tags to spell "jingle" or other desired words. Spray the tags with the matte finish. Let dry.
3 On a protected surface secure one silver eyelet on each tag using an eyelet setter and hammer.
4 Attach a silver jump ring to each jingle bell using long-nose pliers.
5 Cut an 8-inch piece of ribbon for each tag and jingle bell. Fold each 8-inch piece of ribbon in half to make a loop. Push the loop through the eyelet hole from the back side of the tag and feed the ribbon ends through the loop. Follow the same procedure to loop the jingle bells.
6 Space each bell and letter approximately 1½ inches apart on the garland. Fold ribbon ends over garland and insert a brad through the ribbon

layers. Coil each brad end against the back of ribbons to secure using round-nose pliers.

Tissued Treasures

shown on page 98

WHAT YOU NEED
Scissors
Tissue paper, solid or patterned,
    in red, white, and black
18-gauge wire
White matte-finish ornaments
Paintbrush
Matte decoupage medium, such as
    Mod Podge

HERE'S HOW
1 Cut assorted shapes, such as squares, rectangles, and triangles, from the various tissue papers.
2 Cut a piece of wire for each ornament. Bend a hook on each end of the wire and attach the wire to the ornament top to use as a hanger for drying.
3 Brush decoupage medium on one ornament at a time. Add desired tissue paper pieces to the wet surface and coat with another layer of decoupage medium. Hang to dry.

Bead-Berry Ornaments

shown on page 99

WHAT YOU NEED

Floral or other clay
See-through stones
Soft fabric paint, such as Tulip, in
    red, jade, and white; paintbrush
Glass and bead adhesive, such as
    Aleene's Slick Surfaces
Satin ornaments in red and green
Silver three-dimensional paint
    glitter

HERE'S HOW

1 Roll and pull clay into a long straight line. Turn stones upside down and secure in clay. Paint the bottoms of the stones with red or jade fabric paint. Let the paint dry.

2 Cover the bottom of each stone with white fabric paint. Let dry thoroughly.

3 Adhere the stones to the ornament using the glass and bead adhesive. Apply stones to one-third of the ornament at a time. Wait until dry before applying stones to the next area.

4 Apply small dabs of silver glitter paint to the top surface of each stone. Apply to one section at a time. Wait until dry before moving to the next section. Let the paint dry.

Miniature Packages

shown on page 100

WHAT YOU NEED

Wrapping paper, tissue, and
    decorative paper scraps
3 miniature craft boxes in
    different sizes
Glue stick; scissors
Thin ribbon
Small jingle bells, optional
7-inch-long piece of gold cord
    for hanging

HERE'S HOW

1 Select a combination of papers to wrap boxes. Use contrasting papers for each lid and base pair.

2 Cover the outside of the lid or base with glue stick. Place the lid top or base onto the wrong side of the selected paper piece. Pull the sides of the paper up to cover the long sides of the box. Pull the paper up over the short sides of the base. Make diagonal folds at the corners as if wrapping a present. Trim off the paper ends so that only a quarter inch of excess paper remains above top edge. Fold and tuck the ends over the rim into the lid or base. If necessary, apply a little glue to the inside of the lid or base to hold the paper in place. Continue working in this fashion until all lids and bases are covered. Put lids on bases.

3 Stack the boxes and tie them together with a ribbon, forming ends into a bow. If desired, thread jingle bells through the ribbon ends before forming the bow. To make a hanging loop, thread one end of the gold cord under the ribbon bow; knot the ends together.

Star Cornucopias

shown on page 101

WHAT YOU NEED
  Tracing paper
  Pencil
  Scissors
  Decorative papers
  Thick white crafts glue
  Crafts knife
  12-inch piece of thin gold ribbon

HERE'S HOW
1 Trace the pattern, *below,* onto tracing paper and cut out. Trace around the pattern onto the wrong side of the decorative paper. Score and fold along the pattern lines.
2 Cut five triangle star points out of a contrasting decorative paper. Glue them to the wrong side of the top star points. Apply glue to the right side of the flap; then tuck it behind the first cornucopia point. With a crafts knife, cut slits below two star points opposite each other on the cornucopia.
3 For the handle first knot one end of a foot-long ribbon. Then thread the other end in through one slit and out through the other. Knot the end to hold the handle in place.

Star Cornucopias Full-Size Pattern

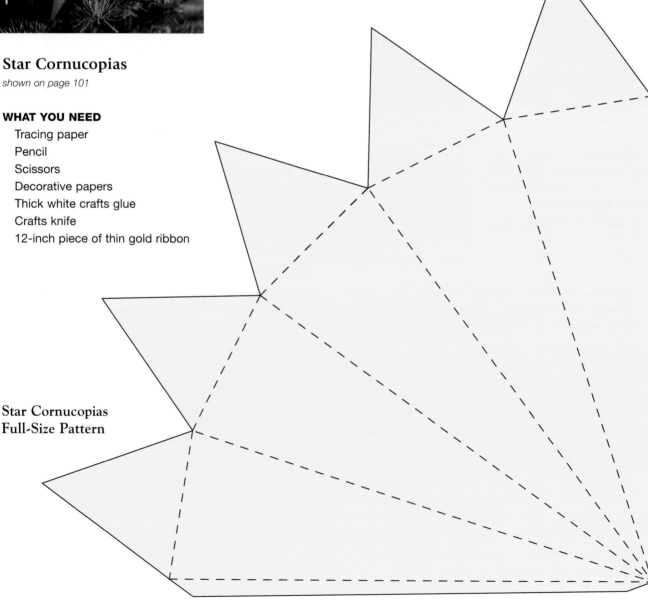

Ribbon-Wrapped Glass Ornaments

shown on page 103

WHAT YOU NEED

Cube-shape glass ornament
Double-sided craft tape sized to
   match the width of the selected
   ribbon
½-inch patterned velvet ribbon
Scissors
White glitter
Artificial evergreen branch
Wire cutters
Artificial snow, such as Aleene's
   True Snow
Glue brush
¼-inch-wide ribbon
Darning needle

HERE'S HOW

1 Remove the metal cap from the top of the ornament and pull out the center bent wire hanger; set both aside.
2 Wrap double-sided craft tape around the center of the glass and press it flat. Peel off the protective backing and wrap the ribbon around the exposed adhesive. Cut the ribbon where it begins to overlap. If necessary use another small piece of double-sided tape to anchor the cut end flat against the mounted ribbon.
3 Pour a small amount of white glitter into the ornament top until the base is almost covered. Replace the metal cap over the top of the ornament.
4 Place the center of a 3-inch section of evergreen over the top of the cap. Thread the wire hanger back through the holes in the metal cap, trapping the evergreen in place. Brush artificial snow onto the tips of the evergreen. Let the snow dry completely.

5 Thread a hanging ribbon through the top of the wire hanger (you may choose to thread the ribbon end through a darning needle first and push the needle through the narrow opening). Bring the ribbon ends together and tie them in an overhand knot.

Vintage Images

shown on page 102

WHAT YOU NEED

Vintage family photographs or
   black and white copies
Scissors
Small silver or gold frames with
   openings at edges
Assortment of gold and silver
   bracelets

HERE'S HOW

1 Use vintage family photos or photocopy the originals, reducing the size if necessary. Trim to fit into frames. Place photos in frames.
2 To hang, thread the bracelets through the open areas on the frame. Secure the clasp.
3 Hang the framed photos on the tree.

Polka-Dot Mushrooms

shown on page 105

WHAT YOU NEED

Plastic foam egg
Serrated plastic knife
Small safety pin
White air-dry modeling clay, such
    as Crayola Model Magic
Red and tan acrylic paint
Paintbrush; red colored sand
Metallic red elastic

HERE'S HOW

1 Use a serrated knife to cut a plastic foam egg shape in half. You can use either half of the cut egg as your mushroom cap, depending on your shape preference. One will be tall and narrow, and the other shorter and wider.
2 Insert a small safety pin, open end first, into the center top of the selected foam mushroom cap. The round safety pin end should stick out above the foam and will become the ornament hanger.
3 Flatten a plum-size ball of air-dry clay and stretch it over the mushroom cap, allowing the safety pin to break through the clay. Bring the clay edges together at the base of the cap and form the excess clay into a stem. Use your fingertips to pinch a fluted collar around the top of the stem. Let the mushroom dry.
4 Brush tan-color acrylic paint under the mushroom cap and stem. After the stem paint has dried, brush red paint over the mushroom cap. Leave circles of the clay unpainted to create a spotted pattern. Working over a small bowl pour red colored sand over the wet red paint. Let dry.
5 Thread a length of metallic elastic through the hole in the pin end, bring the elastic ends together, and tie them in an overhand knot.

Sew-Merry Tree Trims

shown on page 104

WHAT YOU NEED

Assortment of chenille trims in
    bright colors
Hot-glue gun and glue sticks
Frosted glass ball ornaments
Scissors; bright buttons
Ruler
Thread on wood spools
Plastic belt buckles to coordinate
    with chenille and buttons

HERE'S HOW

1 Work with uncut chenille trim directly off the spool.
2 *For the spiral ornament* glue the chenille end just below the metal ring of the ornament. Wrap or spiral the chenille around the ornament, gluing the trim at 1-inch intervals. Cut the chenille off the spool when finished or when a change of colors is needed.
3 *For the spotted ornament* hot-glue buttons randomly onto the ornament.

Hot-glue a contrasting strip of chenille around each button.
4 *To finish the ornaments* cover the metal rims with chenille. Then thread a 7-inch length of chenille through each hanger and tie the ends into a bow.
5 *To make the spool ornaments* thread a 7-inch length of chenille through the center hole and tie the ends into a bow.
6 *To make the buckle garland* thread buckles onto chenille trim or rickrack, spacing approximately 8 inches apart. For buckle trims simply tie onto tree with loops of chenille trim.
7 *To make the topper* cut four 16-inch lengths of desired color of chenille trim. Thread one length through a large button. Align the remaining three chenille trims with the trim on the button and tie them into a bow.
8 To add more color to the branches, tie small chenille trim bows directly onto the branch ends.

Cleverly Colored Ornaments

shown on page 106

WHAT YOU NEED

    Glass ornaments
    Rubbing alcohol
    Paper towels
    Scissors
    Masking tape
    Wire; ruler
    Side cutters
    Newspapers
    Krylon Reactions Paint Styling
        Spray
    Spray paint, such as Krylon Home
        Decor Latex Spray, in kiwi green,
        teal, freesia, and maize
    Stained glass spray paint, such as
        Krylon Stained Glass Color, in
        red, yellow and purple
    Gold metallic spray paint
    Clear coat spray; crafts knife
    Cotton swabs and fingernail polish
        remover (optional)
    18 kt gold leafing pen, such as
        Krylon

HERE'S HOW

1 Clean ornaments with rubbing alcohol and paper towels. Let dry.
2 Cut squares and rectangles out of masking tape. Apply to ornaments and gently rub down all of the edges.
3 Cut wire approximately 10 inches long using side cutters. Bend a hook on

each end of the wire for hanging the ornaments while they are drying.
4 In a well-ventilated work area, cover the surface with newspapers. Spray ornaments one at a time with the Reactions spray paint, referring to the manufacturer's instructions. Immediately follow with various home decor latex sprays, stained glass sprays, and metallic paint. The colors will blend together in beautiful combinations. Experiment with more or less Reactions spray to vary the results. Let the ornaments dry.
5 Spray the ornaments with two coats of clear spray. Let dry.
6 Before removing the masking tape from the ornaments, gently score the edges of the tape with a crafts knife to help prevent paint from pulling away with the tape. Gently scrape off any paint from the ornament that may have leaked under the masking tape (or you can remove it with cotton swabs and fingernail polish remover).
7 Highlight each clear glass square or rectangle with a gold leafing pen. Let it dry.

Graphic Garland

shown on page 107

WHAT YOU NEED

    Scissors and ruler (optional)
    2-inch circle paper punch (optional)

    Square paper punch in 2-inch and
        ⅝-inch sizes (optional)
    Pink and blue pastel muted
        scrapbook paper
    Brushed gold scrapbook paper
    Double-sided tape
    18 kt gold leafing pen, such as
        Krylon
    ⅛-inch hole punch
    Gold scrapbook eyelets
    Eyelet setter and hammer
    Gold polyester cording
    Hot-glue gun and glue sticks
    Gold hoop earring wires
    Gold 6 mm beads
    Long-nose pliers

HERE'S HOW

1 Cut or punch out 2-inch circles and squares from pastel scrapbook paper. Cut or punch out ⅝-inch squares from gold scrapbook paper.
2 Adhere pairs of large squares and circles together back-to-back using double-sided tape. Adhere small gold squares to the fronts (and backs if desired) of each large square and circle using double-sided tape.
3 Edge each large square and circle with leafing pen. Punch a hole in the top of each square and circle. On a protected surface, apply an eyelet and set it with an eyelet setter and hammer.
4 Space out small loops in gold cording approximately 2 inches apart. Hot-glue the loops in place. Attach the large squares and circles to the cording loops using the gold hoop earring wires. Add a gold bead to each wire. Bend the tip of the straight end of each hoop earring up ¹⁄₁₆ inch using long-nose pliers. This will allow it to catch and fasten in the other end of the earring wire.

'tis better to give

Chers!

This year, share your talents with everyone on your gift list. They'll be extra thankful to receive a unique handmade reminder of you.

You'll have grounds for celebration with these thoughtful presents. Give guests a memento of your holiday coffee party by presenting them with a vintage-style **Cup-O-Coffee,** *opposite.* The **Chocolate-Dipped Silver-Spoon Stirrers,** *left,* are sweet treats for coffee lovers. To give any gift in style, place it in a **Beribboned Jewel Box,** *above,* topped with organza and variegated ribbons. Instructions are on *page 125.*

To give a gift that will be cherished forever, be creative with family photos. Black and white copies create **Trifold Greetings** that pop with colored pencil accents. The **Finial Photo Holders,** *opposite*, can be made to coordinate with any decor, depending on the paints and embellishments you choose. Instructions are on *page 126*.

Simple shapes and bold, unexpected colors team up for a graphic, contemporary look. Start with small artist's canvases to paint a **Funky Tree Trio** as easy as paint by number. The finished artwork is deep enough to sit on a shelf or it can hang as a grouping on a wall. Instructions and patterns are on *page 127*.

With just a few simple steps, you can make gifts to give with love to all your family members. **Photo Blocks,** made from home center trim pieces, are an artistic way to show off favorite snapshots. To reward your pooch, put together a **Chic Dog Toy Basket,** *opposite*, and fill it with new playthings. Instructions are on *pages 128–129*.

Convenient carryalls are funky and functional. **Cigar Box** and **Spell-It-Out Purses,** shown *opposite*, are right with the times touting imaginative trims. For the sweet tooth on your gift list, decorate a **Holiday Spice Jar Set** to hold a selection of candies in Christmas colors. Instructions are on *pages 129–130.*

Pamper someone special with easy-to-knit sensations that ward off winter's chill. **Stadium Mittens** show off a handsome field of texture in two colors of wool. Flowing fringes finish the ends of a **So-Hip Checked Scarf**— a stylish accessory for the season. Instructions are on *pages 130–131*.

Cup-O-Coffee

shown on page 114

WHAT YOU NEED

Vintage coffee cup and saucer
Chocolate-covered espresso
  beans
Scissors
Off-white card stock; paper punch
Gold fine-line marking pen
Clear cellophane; gold cord

HERE'S HOW

1 Fill the coffee cup with beans.
2 Cut a small tag from card stock. Punch a hole in one end. Write desired message on the tag.
3 Cover the cup with cellophane. Tie cord around the top of the cup, threading the tag onto the cord.

Chocolate-Dipped Silver-Spoon Stirrers

shown on page 115

WHAT YOU NEED

Microwave-safe bowls
Chocolate and white almond bark

Silver spoon; waxed paper
Table knife; clear cellophane
Gold cord

HERE'S HOW

1 In a microwave-safe bowl melt chocolate in the microwave set on medium setting, watching carefully.
2 Dip the tip of each spoon scoop in chocolate. Set on waxed paper until firm.
3 In a microwave-safe bowl melt the almond bark in the microwave set on medium setting, watching carefully. Dip a knife into the melted almond bark; drizzle on the chocolate-dipped spoon. Let set.
4 Wrap spoon in cellophane; secure with cord tied around the handle.

Beribboned Jewel Box

shown on page 115

WHAT YOU NEED

Newspapers
4½x3x2½-inch hinged wood box
Spray acrylic sealer
Organza ribbons in a variety of
  widths in mauve, pink, tan, ivory,
  hunter green, and red
Scissors; thick white crafts glue
Disposable foam brush
Aluminum foil
¼ yard of moiré taffeta lining fabric
  (optional)
½ yard of 1.4 mm red variegated
  ribbon

Ruler
Red sewing thread and needle
Hot-glue gun and glue sticks
3 artificial silver flower stamens

HERE'S HOW

1 In a well-ventilated work area, cover work surface with newspapers. Spray the box inside and out with acrylic sealer. Set the box aside.
2 Plan the arrangement of organza ribbons for the plaid design with the bottom layer consisting of horizontal ribbons and the top layer of vertical ribbons.
3 Thin glue with water and brush onto lid. When the glue becomes tacky, apply the layer of horizontal ribbons over the lid, smoothing them from side to side. Let dry.
4 Apply thinned glue over the lid again. In the same manner apply the remaining ribbons from front to back. Also adhere a length of ribbon around all four sides of lid. Let dry.
5 Apply two more coats of thinned glue to the lid, letting the medium dry between coats. Prop the lid open with foil to prevent sealing it closed.
6 Glue a band of ribbon around each foot of the box. Apply a coat of thinned glue to the exterior box sides and bottom. Line the box with the taffeta fabric if desired.
7 For each flower cut a 5½-inch-long piece of variegated ribbon. Work gathering stitches around three sides of the ribbon, leaving one long side ungathered. Pull the thread tightly to gather the stitches, coiling the ribbon around itself as you gather; secure with backstitches. Make three flowers.
8 Hot-glue stamens to the center of each flower. Tie two or three bows from the desired organza ribbons. Hot-glue the bows and flowers to the lid.

Trifold Greetings

shown on page 116

WHAT YOU NEED
- Ruler
- Envelope
- Pencil
- White card stock
- Scissors or paper trimmer
- Photographs
- Black and white copier
- Circle cutter (optional)
- Fine-line marking pen
- Glue stick
- Colored pencils

HERE'S HOW

1 Measure an envelope and draw a rectangle the same height and three times wider on white card stock. Cut out and trifold the rectangle.

2 Make black and white photocopies of snapshots. Trim photos to fit the card if necessary. If desired, crop photos using a circle cutter. Arrange and glue the photos on the trifold card. Write sentiments where desired using a fine-line marking pen.

3 Tint select portions of the photos using colored pencils.

Finial Photo Holders

shown on page 117

WHAT YOU NEED
- Wood finials
- Krylon interior/exterior semiflat black spray paint; masking tape
- Stone texture paint, such as Krylon's Make It Stone! Textured Paint, in Mediterranean Reef
- Krylon metallic spray paints in silver, gold, and copper
- Side cutters
- 18-gauge annealed wire; ruler
- Round-nose pliers; hand drill; bit
- Strong adhesive, such as Quick Grip
- Silver 8 mm jump rings
- Clear acrylic crystals
- Silver eye pins; long-nose pliers
- Silver beads
- Stone Kit in magenta and gold, such as Krylon Mystique
- Gold chain; 6 mm gold jump rings
- Assorted beads in magenta and gold
- Gold head pin

HERE'S HOW

1 *For the green/black/silver holder,* on a protected surface in a well-ventilated work area, spray finial black. Let dry. Carefully mask off all areas except where the Mediterranean Reef stone paint is to go. Apply the stone paint. Let dry. Mask off all areas except where the silver paint is to go. Apply silver paint. Let dry.

2 Using side cutters, cut three pieces of annealed wire each 14 inches long. Coil the wires using round-nose pliers. Cut one piece of wire 5 inches long. Wrap it around the base of the wires to secure. Drill a hole in the top of the finial for the wires. Apply strong adhesive to the bottom of the wires and insert into the finial. Let dry.

3 Attach one silver 8 mm jump ring to each acrylic crystal. Attach to silver eye pin using long-nose pliers. Thread one silver bead onto each eye pin and bend the open wire end into a loop using round-nose pliers. Thread onto the lower two coils of wire.

4 *For the magenta/gold/copper holder,* carefully mask off all areas except where the magenta and gold stone paint is to go. On a protected surface apply the Mystique base coat and subsequent paints according to manufacturer's directions. Mask off all areas except where the copper paint is to go. Apply copper paint. Let dry. Mask off all areas except where the gold paint is to go. Apply gold paint. Let dry.

5 Using side cutter, cut three pieces of annealed wire each 14 inches long. Coil the wires using round-nose pliers. Cut one piece of wire 5 inches long. Wrap it around the base of the wires to secure. Drill a hole in the top of the finial for the wires. Apply strong adhesive to the bottom of the wires and insert into the finial. Let dry.

6 Cut a piece of gold chain to fit around the base of the finial. Connect the chain together with a gold jump ring using long-nose pliers. Thread magenta and gold beads onto a head pin. Cut off excess, leaving ¼ inch wire on end. Bend the wire end into a loop using round-nose pliers. Attach beaded head pin to chain using a jump ring.

Funky Tree Trio

shown on pages 118–119

WHAT YOU NEED

Paintbrushes

Gesso, such as Delta Ceramcoat

5×7 gallery canvas frames

Acrylic paints in red, eggplant, bright yellow, green, opaque blue, and white

Tracing paper; pencil

Scissors

Carbon paper

Masking tape

18 kt gold leafing pen, such as Krylon

Newspapers

Satin interior spray varnish

HERE'S HOW

1 Brush a coat of Gesso on the canvas. Let dry.

2 Brush eggplant acrylic paint onto the canvas. While the paint is still wet, dip a clean brush into water and then into white paint and brush it over the eggplant paint to form a streaked/mixed look. If too much white paint is applied, simply wipe off the excess with a paper towel. Let dry.

3 Trace the patterns, *below,* and cut them out. Lay the tree patterns over carbon paper cut to fit the canvases. Tape the papers in place with masking tape. Trace the patterns firmly with a pencil.

4 Paint the trees using the red, bright yellow, green, and opaque blue. Let dry.

5 Outline the trees with the leafing pen. Dot the background of the trees with the gold pen. Let dry.

6 In a well-ventilated work area, cover the work surface with newspapers. Spray the paintings with two coats of varnish, allowing to dry between coats. Let dry.

**Funky Tree Trio
Full-Size Patterns
(enlarge to fit desired
canvas size)**

Chic Dog Toy Basket
shown on page 121

WHAT YOU NEED
Pencil
2×3-inch wood rectangles
Drill and bit; sandpaper
All-purpose sealer
Paintbrush
Acrylic paints in mustard and
   light ivory
Checkerboard stencil, such as
   Rubber Stampede A2233C
Stencil brush
Black paint pen
Satin interior/exterior varnish
Wicker basket
⅛-inch-wide black ribbon
Ruler; scissors

HERE'S HOW
1 Mark the top corners of each wood rectangle to drill holes for hanging. Drill holes on protected surface. Sand each rectangle.
2 Apply sealer to the wood according to manufacturer's directions. Let dry.
3 Brush on two coats of light ivory paint, allowing to dry between coats.
4 Lay checkerboard stencil over rectangle. Apply mustard paint with stencil brush. Let dry and apply a second coat of mustard paint. Repeat for each rectangle.
5 Using a black paint pen, write out the following words on the rectangles:

Photo Blocks
shown on page 120

WHAT YOU NEED
Photos (Antique sepia-tone or
   black and white images work
   well. You can convert many
   photos to black and white or
   brown tone at do-it-yourself
   photo centers.)
Paper trimmer
Wood trim pieces (available
   in the trim section at home
   center stores)
Acrylic paints in desired colors
Paintbrush
Spray adhesive
Gold highlighting medium,
   such as Rub 'n' Buff
Fine sandpaper
Tack cloth

HERE'S HOW
1 Trim the photos to fit onto the smooth areas of the wood trim pieces. Set the trimmed photos aside.
2 Paint each of the wood pieces with one coat of acrylic paint in desired colors. Let the paint dry.
3 In a well-ventilated work area, spray the back side of the photos with spray adhesive; mount onto the painted pieces of wood trim.
4 Place a very small amount of gold highlighting medium on a finger and rub onto the wood to highlight until the desired look is achieved.
5 Use fine sandpaper to sand edges and corners where the photo is attached to give it a subtle worn effect. Sand the raised areas on wood pieces. Wipe off the dust with a tack cloth.

Woof woof (American English)
Vou vou (Danish/Swedish)
Ouah-ouah (French)
Guau guau (Spanish)
Wau wau (German)

Varnish the rectangles and let dry.

6 Cut two 5-inch-long pieces of black ribbon for each rectangle. Thread ribbon through holes and wicker of basket. Knot ribbons on the inside of the basket.

Cigar Box Purse

shown on page 122

WHAT YOU NEED

Newspapers
Oil-base varnish
Tall cigar box purse, such as
    Plaid Enterprises
Paintbrush
Fine sandpaper
Assorted scrapbook washers
Assorted rondelle beads in gold
    and silver
3 mm beads in gold and silver
Pencil; straight pin
Crafts knife
20-gauge brass wire
Wire cutters; ruler
Small buttons
Long-nose pliers

2-inch-long gold eye pin
Round-nose pliers
Pendant drop bead
6 mm gold jump rings
Ball and chain with end

HERE'S HOW

1 Cover work surface with newspaper and apply the first coat of varnish to cigar box purse using a paintbrush. Let the varnish dry. Lightly sand before applying the second coat of varnish. Let it dry.

2 Lay out washers on the front lid of cigar box purse. Layer washers and beads as desired. Mark the center of each stack on the box using a pencil. Using a straight pin, puncture a hole in each center. Enlarge the holes if necessary by using a crafts knife.

3 To attach the washers and beads, cut a 4-inch piece of wire for hole center using wire cutters. Thread wire through the center of each bead and bend the wire ends together. Thread the wire ends through the remaining washers, through the purse hole center, and through two holes of a button on the inside of the lid. Twist the wires together using long-nose pliers. Snip off the excess wire and bend the wire ends into one of the buttonholes.

4 Thread assorted beads and washers on eye pin. Snip off excess wire, leaving ¼-inch length on the end. Bend end into a loop using round-nose pliers. Attach a pendant drop bead to bottom of eye pin loop using long-nose pliers and a jump ring. Attach to the ball and chain pendant on the purse handle with a jump ring.

Spell-It-Out Purse

shown on page 122

WHAT YOU NEED

Scissors
Black Velcro
Fabric purse of your choice
Permanent fabric adhesive, such
    as Beacon Fabric-Tac
Black thread; sewing needle
Colorful letters cut from magazines
Double-sided tape
Newspaper
Matte finish spray, such as Krylon

HERE'S HOW

1 Cut a square piece of Velcro (loop or thick soft side) to fit the front side of the fabric purse. Apply fabric adhesive to the back of the Velcro piece and adhere to purse. Let dry.

2 Using black thread and a needle, hand-sew the four corners of the Velcro material down for added durability.

3 Apply magazine letters to the back side of the opposing Velcro (the thin hook side) using double-sided tape. Lay the magazine letters on a piece of newspaper and apply two thin coats of finish spray, allowing drying time between coats. Arrange the magazine letters on Velcro attached to purse.

Holiday Spice Jar Set

shown on page 123

WHAT YOU NEED

- Chrome-top spice jars
- Rubbing alcohol
- Paper towels
- Double-sided tape; scissors
- Holiday bottle caps, such as Li'l Davis Designs (available in scrapbooking stores)
- Tiny glass marbles in red, green, and silver (available in scrapbooking stores)
- Small cup
- Small container
- Ultrafine glitter in red, green, and silver
- ⅜-inch ribbon in red and green
- 3×6-inch silver-tone organizer

HERE'S HOW

1 Empty and clean spice jars. Wipe jar lids with rubbing alcohol and paper towels. Let dry.

2 Apply strips of double-sided tape to jar lid. Trim off the excess tape around the jar lid. Peel tape backing off lid. Peel tape backing off bottle cap adhesive (cap comes with adhesive insert). Center bottle cap over lid and press into place.

3 Pour one color of tiny marbles into small cup. Hold lid over small container and gently pour tiny marbles over lid. Pour the excess marbles back into the original bag.

4 Sprinkle ultrafine glitter in a matching color over the lid to fill in any spaces. Shake off excess glitter. Repeat this procedure for the other colors.

5 Cut ribbon to fit around lid of jars. Fold under one end of each ribbon using double-sided tape. Tape the unfolded end of ribbon to jar lid and wrap ribbon around lid. Tape the folded end of ribbon to the other end using tape. Repeat for each jar. With double-sided tape, tape a long piece of ribbon around the base of silver organizer (see *page 123*) using the same method as the jar lids. Fill jars with colorful treats.

Stadium Mittens

shown on page 124

SKILL LEVEL: Easy

SIZE: Adult size S (M, L)

FINISHED MEASUREMENTS:

Width: 3½" (4¼", 5")
Length: 10½" (11½", 12")

WHAT YOU NEED

- Lion Brand, Wool-Ease Chunky, Article #630, 80% acrylic/20% wool yarn (153 yards per ball): 1 ball each of Foliage (187) for MC and Evergreen (180) for Color A
- Size 6 (4.25mm) knitting needles or size needed to obtain gauge
- Size 4 (3.5mm) knitting needles
- Yarn needle
- 2 ring-type stitch markers

GAUGE:

In St st (k RS rows, p WS rows) with larger needles, 16 sts and 23 rows = 4"/10cm.

TAKE TIME TO CHECK YOUR GAUGE.

SPECIAL ABBREVIATIONS:

M1: To make 1 st, lift the horizontal bar between right and left needles onto the left needle, and k into back of this lp.
Ssk: Slip next 2 sts knitwise, one at a time, to right-hand needle; insert tip of left-hand needle into fronts of these 2 sts and k tog.
Pm: Place a marker.

STITCHES USED:

Body Pattern (a multiple of 2 sts + 1 st; a rep of 4 rows)
Row 1 (WS): Purl.
Row 2: * K1, p1; rep from * across, ending k1.
Row 3: * P1, k1; rep from * across, ending p1.
Row 4: Knit.
Rows 1–4 for Body Pattern.

INSTRUCTIONS:

RIGHT MITTEN

Cuff

With Color A and smaller needles, cast on 25 (31, 37) sts. K 1 row. * With MC, work Rows 1–4 of Body Pattern; with A, work Rows 1–4 of Body Pattern. Rep from * twice more.

Setup for Body Pattern

With larger needles and MC, p.
Next Row: Work Body Pattern on first 13 (16, 19) sts, M1, k1, M1, k to end of row—27 (33, 39) sts. Next Row: P14 (17, 20), work Row 3 of Body Pattern to end. Pattern is now set. Work 2 (2, 4) more rows as est.

Thumb

Row 1 (RS): Work est pattern on first 13 (16, 19) sts, pm, M1, k1, M1, pm, pattern to end of row.

Row 2: Work pattern across.

Row 3: Work to marker, slip marker, M1, k to marker, M1, work to end of row. Rep Rows 2–3 until there are 13 (13, 15) sts between markers. Work 1 row even. Next Row: Work across, removing markers and placing thumb sts onto a spare strand of yarn. Cont in est patterns on the 26 (32, 38) sts until piece measures approx 9½" (10", 10½") from beg, ending with a WS row and placing a marker after the 13th (16th, 19th) st.

Top Shaping

Row 1 (RS): Ssk, work to 2 sts before marker, k2tog, sl marker, ssk, work to last 2 sts, k2tog.

Row 2: Work pat across. Rep last 2 rows until 18 (20, 22) sts rem. (K2tog) across—9 (10, 11) sts. Leaving a long tail, cut yarn.

Closure

Thread tail into yarn needle. Beg with the last st on needle, take yarn back through rem sts twice. Pull up to close opening. Leave tail for joining sides.

Thumb

With RS facing, return sts to larger needle. Join MC and k 13 (13, 15).

Next Row: P 5 (5, 6), p2tog, p 6 (6, 7). Work 6 more St st rows on the 12 (12, 14) sts. (K2tog) across. Rep Closure as for Top. Join thumb seam. Darn opening. Weave in loose end on WS of fabric.

FINISHING

Join side seam.

LEFT MITTEN

Work Cuff as for Right Mitten.

Setup for Body Pattern

With larger needles and MC, p. **Next Row:** K11 (14, 17), pm. M1, k1, M1, pm, work Body Pattern to end—27 (33, 39) sts. **Next Row:** Work Body Pattern Row 3 on 13 (16, 19) sts, p to end. Pattern is

now set. Work 2 (2, 4) more rows as est. Complete as for Right Mitten.

So-Hip Checked Scarf

shown on page 124

SKILL LEVEL: Easy

SIZE: Approximately 7"×57"

WHAT YOU NEED

Lion Brand, Kool Wool, 50% merino wool/50% acrylic, chunk-weight yarn (60 yards per ball): 3 balls of Khaky (124) for Color A and 2 balls of Grass (130) for Color B

Size 10½ (6.5 mm) knitting needles or size needed to obtain gauge

Size K/10½ (6.5 mm) crochet hook

GAUGE:

In Color Pattern, 14 sts and 15 rows = 4"/10 cm.

TAKE TIME TO CHECK YOUR GAUGE.

SPECIAL ABBREVIATIONS:

Sl 1: Slip next stitch purlwise and with yarn on WS of fabric.

Sl 3: Slip next 3 stitches purlwise and with yarn on WS of fabric.

STITCHES USED:

Color Pattern (a multiple of 4 sts + 1 st; a rep of 8 rows)

Row 1 (WS): With A, k1, p across, ending k1.

Row 2: With B, k1, sl 1; * k1, sl 3; rep from * across, ending k1, sl 1, k1.

Row 3: With B, k1; * p3, sl 1; rep from * across, ending p3, k1.

Row 4: With A, k2; * sl 1, k3; rep from * across, ending sl 1, k2.

Row 5: As Row 1.

Row 6: With B, k1; * sl 3, k1; rep from * across.

Row 7: With B, k1, p1; * sl 1, p3; rep from * across, ending sl 1, p1, k1.

Row 8: With A, k4; * sl 1, k3, rep from * across, ending k1.

Rep Rows 1–8 for Color Pattern.

INSTRUCTIONS:

With Color A, cast on 25 sts. Work Color Pattern to approx 57" from beg, ending with Row 1 or Row 5. Bind off. Block scarf to measurements.

FRINGE

Cut 3 strands of A measuring 10" each. Fold in half to form a loop. With WS of fabric facing and crochet hook, take loop through first st at right edge. Take ends through loop and pull up to tighten. Alternating the colors, add 11 fringe along each edge. Trim ends.

COMMON ABBREVIATIONS

approx	approximately
beg	begin(ning)
cont	continue
dec	decrease
est	established
inc	increase
k	knit
k2tog	knit 2 together
lp	loop
M1	make one stitch
MC	main color
pat	pattern
p	purl
rem	remain(s)(ing)
rep	repeat
RS	right side
sl	slip
ssk	slip, slip, knit
st(s)	stitch(es)
St st	stockinette stitch
tog	together
WS	wrong side

rich in tradition

Whether you anticipate the familiar joy of Christmas red and green or comforting holiday motifs, you'll love this chapter brimming with new twists.

Sprinkle your home with touches of Christmas red this holiday season. The **Elegant Embossed Clay Candle Cups**, *left*, are grooved with swirls and can be edged in gold for extra sparkle. The **Garland of Goodies** features star-shape cookies strung between a traditional popcorn-and-cranberry garland. Instructions are on *page 144*.

Rich with holiday hues, this duo is a wonderful example of traditional decor with fresh perspectives. **Poinsettia Banister Baskets**, *opposite*, are bursting with lush red silk poinsettias, delicate berries, and a selection of Christmas picks. The **Pretty Patched Wreath** showcases rustic embroidery stitches with holiday charm accents. Instructions are on *pages 144–145*.

Flowers and fruit are naturals in traditional holiday decorating. For an extraordinary package topper, a **Beaded Poinsettia Bow** is a grand statement. To provide an aromatic display, arrange **Studded Pomanders,** *opposite*, atop a nut-filled bowl for a Southern-style centerpiece. Instructions are on *pages 145–146.*

Holiday wreaths and garlands are limited only by your imagination.

Fresh green apples and pears, clustered in twos and threes,

highlight the **Stunning Staircase Garland,** *opposite*. Use piñon

cones with a woodlike appearance to create a **Piñon Cone Wreath**

surrounded by magnolia leaves. Instructions are on *page 146*.

Combine the rustic with the elegant for eyecatching home accents. To store seasonal cards or candies, craft a **Christmas Deer Box** from textured papers. Bring glistening gold to the dining table by dressing dark red tapers with dots of sealing wax on **Delightfully Dotted Tapers,** *opposite*. Instructions and pattern are on *pages 146–147.*

This fireside arrangement limits its seasonal palette to a range of warm

winter whites and soft woodsy browns and reds. The **Personalized Pillow,**

opposite, features a monogrammed linen napkin stitched to the quilted front.

Pinecones, seedpods, fruit, and jingle bells create an engaging parade of

tones and textures along a **Christmas Jubilee Garland.** Instructions are

on *page 147*.

Elegant Embossed Clay Candle Cups

shown on pages 132–133

WHAT YOU NEED

Light embossing aluminum, such
   as Aluminum ArtEmboss metal
Scissors
Dark pink pillar candles; tape
Polymer clay in red and fuchsia
Clay roller or dedicated pasta
   machine for clay (optional)
Cornstarch and freezer paper
   (optional); clay texture sheets,
   such as Polyform Products'
   Dancing Spirals and Party Favors
Pigment ink pads, such as Color
   Box Cat's Eye, in gold and silver
Crafts knife; all-purpose permanent
   adhesive, such as Quick Grip
Small ball chain; gold mini brads
Side cutters

HERE'S HOW

1 Make candle collar forms by cutting
a strip of aluminum long enough to
wrap around each candle. Make the
aluminum strips taller than each clay
collar. Tape the aluminum strip from
the inside so no tape is exposed, and
leave a little space for the form to slip
on and off the candle.

2 Mix equal parts of red and fuchsia
clays. Condition clay by repeatedly
rolling it with a clay roller or with a
pasta machine. If rolling, use a thin
layer of cornstarch on freezer paper for
the work surface.

3 One at a time, stamp texture sheets
with metallic inks. Press texture sheets
onto rolled-out clay and press down

evenly according to the manufacturer's
directions. Using a crafts knife, cut out
a colorful edge around the textured clay
or cut out extra textured clay images
and add them to the main piece of
textured clay for added dimension.

4 Dust the aluminum forms with
cornstarch before wrapping the textured
clay around them. Bake clay according
to manufacturer's directions. Let cool
five minutes before removing the forms.
Let clay continue to cool.

5 If desired, glue ball chain along the
upper edges of clay collars. Let dry. To
decorate with brads, snip off the ends
and glue the heads to the clay. Let dry.

Garland of Goodies

shown on page 133

WHAT YOU NEED

Royal icing; food coloring
Star-shape purchased cookies
Edible glitter; fresh cranberries
Popcorn; 28-gauge silver wire
½-inch-wide satin ribbon, cut into
   12-inch lengths

HERE'S HOW

1 Tint icing in desired colors with food
coloring. Frost cookies. While frosting
is wet, sprinkle with glitter. Let dry.

2 Alternately string cranberries and
popcorn onto wire. Allow a little slack

at each end for hanging loops. Use a
piece of wire to poke a hole in the top
of each cookie; string a length of ribbon
through each hole. At desired intervals,
slide the cranberry and popcorn apart
slightly; tie the ribbon around the wire.

Poinsettia Banister Baskets

shown on page 134

WHAT YOU NEED

Foam cone 5–6 inches in diameter
   at the base (one cone makes two
   bouquets); marking pen; ruler
Serrated knife; sandpaper
Decoupage medium, such as Mod
   Podge; metallic gold tissue paper
Paintbrush; metallic gold paint
Artificial red poinsettias, red and
   gold berries, and Christmas picks
20-gauge wire; wire cutters
2-inch-wide gold ribbon (3 yards
   per bouquet)

HERE'S HOW

1 On a protected work surface, lay
cone on its side; mark 10 inches from
the widest end. Cut foam at mark using
a knife. Set the cone with the widest
base on the work surface; cut the foam
lengthwise. On each half, make a mark
2 inches from the widest end of the
foam. Cut the foam from the mark
downward toward the center of the

thinnest end of the foam to help form a sharper V in foam. Sand foam smooth.

2 Use decoupage medium to adhere tissue paper to cone bases. Let dry. Brush on metallic gold paint for a deeper color. Let dry.

3 Insert poinsettias, berries, and picks into bases. Twist wires on the back to form two loops. Cut two 1½-yard lengths of ribbon for each cone; tie to each wire loop.

4 Wrap banister with ribbon. Tie cones onto banister; make a large bow on back. Add picks near each cone.

Pretty-Patch Wreath

shown on page 135

WHAT YOU NEED

24-inch square of batiste
⅛ to ¼ yard each of 15 different
    red, green, and white fabrics
Fabric marking pen
Assorted embroidery threads, perle
    cotton, and novelty threads in
    red, green, and white
Sewing needle; thread; batting
2½ yards of sew-in red piping cord
    (lightweight cotton fabric)
24-inch square of red felt; polyfil
Assorted heart and holiday charms
Ribbon
Cabone ring

HERE'S HOW

1 For the crazy patchwork, start in the center of the batiste fabric. Baste five fabrics to batiste, creating a five-sided piece. Right sides together, sew the next fabric piece with ¼-inch seam allowance onto any side. Press the second piece to the right side.

2 Working clockwise, stitch the third piece of fabric in the same manner completely covering the edges of piece one and piece two. Press to right side.

3 Continue working in a clockwise direction around all five sides, trimming excess fabric. Patchwork in this manner covering the batiste fabric.

4 Center and trace a 20-inch circle with a 5-inch center circle onto the patchwork. Work embroidery stitches (see *page 35* for diagrams) covering seams inside the wreath shape. Line patchwork with batting and machine baste on the traced circles.

5 Cut out wreath allowing a ¼-inch seam. Stitch red piping to outside and inside circles.

6 With right sides facing, stitch wreath to red felt around outside edge. Cut out felt 5 inches inside circle. Trim and clip outside circle even. Turn wreath to the right side.

7 Stuff wreath shape with polyfil. Turn under seam allowance on the inside circles and hand-stitch the front patchwork to the felt back. Tack heart and holiday charms to patchwork. Sew a cabone ring onto back side for hanging. Trim wreath with ribbon bow.

Beaded Poinsettia Bow

as shown on page 136

WHAT YOU NEED

Tracing paper; pencil; scissors
Fusible adhesive; felt in red, dark
    green, gold, and light green
Metallic gold sewing machine thread
Sewing thread; needle; 7 metallic
    gold round beads; 7 metallic
    gold cupped flower beads; ribbon

WHAT TO DO

1 Enlarge and trace and cut out the patterns, *below*. Trace patterns on the paper side of fusible adhesive.

2 Fuse the adhesive to red felt; cut out the shapes. Fuse each poinsettia shape to green felt pieces. Trim the green felt just beyond the red edges. Cut the flower center from gold felt.

3 Using metallic gold thread and a decorative sewing machine stitch, outline-stitch along the red leaves.

4 Layer the poinsettias to show all the leaves, with the larger layer beneath. Tack the flower center in place.

5 Using thread and a needle, hand-sew through the flower center and the two layers of leaves, attaching a cupped flower bead and round bead with each stitch. Wrap a ribbon around a package; sew the poinsettia to the ribbon.

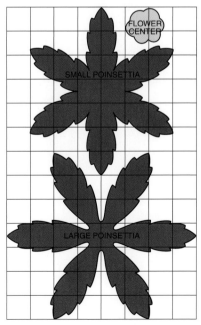

1 Square = 1 Inch

Enlarge at 400%

Studded Pomanders

shown on page 137

WHAT YOU NEED

Oranges
Large sewing needle
Whole cloves
Yellow kumquats
Oval bowl
Nuts
Bay leaves

HERE'S HOW

1 Pierce the desired designs in several oranges using a large needle. Press whole cloves into the needle holes. Poke random holes in the kumquats. Insert cloves into the holes.
2 Fill the bowl with nuts. Nestle the pomanders among the nuts. Tuck sprigs of bay leaves into the arrangement.

Stunning Staircase Garland

shown on page 138

WHAT YOU NEED

Fresh garland
Twine
Burlap and moiré ribbon
Sprigs of ivy and other desired
    greenery

Scissors
Wood floral picks
Green apples
Pears

HERE'S HOW

1 Drape fresh garland around the banister and railing. Secure the garland with pieces of twine.
2 Tuck burlap and moiré ribbons around and over the twine. Insert sprigs of ivy and other greenery, and tie on ample ribbon bows and streamers.
3 Insert wood floral picks into the plumpest parts of the fruit. Tightly wrap the wire end of the pick around the garland, grouping the fruit in twos and threes.

Piñon Cone Wreath

shown on page 139

WHAT YOU NEED

Foam wreath form
Thick white crafts glue
Cardboard ring cut to wreath
    form size; scissors
Piñon cones; floral wire
Magnolia leaves
Wood floral picks
Sprigs of variegated boxwood and
    Hypericum berries

HERE'S HOW

1 To reinforce the foam wreath, glue on the cardboard ring.

2 Cut off the tops of the piñon cones. Use the remaining bases for the wreath.
3 Dip the cut cone ends into glue and attach the cones to the wreath so the bottoms of the cones form the wreath surface. Completely cover the wreath form with cones. For variety glue on a few cones with the cut tops facing up.
4 Wire stems of magnolia leaves to wood floral picks around the outer and inner edges of the wreath. On the outer rim alternate the sides of the leaves that face forward (the top side is green and the underside is gold). To fill in gaps in the wreath, glue or wrap wire around bunched sprigs of boxwood and berries and push the wired bunches into foam.

Christmas Deer Box

shown on page 140

WHAT YOU NEED

Cardboard container
2 tones of green acrylic paint
Sponge; gold glazing gel
Tracing paper; pencil; scissors
Textured paper in brown, cream,
    and red
Porcelain Christmas flowers,
    greens, and berries
Ribbon
Hot-glue gun and glue sticks
Square crocheted doily (optional)

Gold highlighting medium, such as
  Rub 'n' Buff
Thick white crafts glue

HERE'S HOW

1 Paint cardboard container and lid using two tones of green and sponge on the paint until it is blended as desired. Two very different greens, such as a light or bright and a very dark green, result in more contrast. Two similar colors in different hue or intensity will achieve more subtle mottling. Let dry.
2 Dab a small amount of gold glazing gel onto sponge and dab lightly onto green surface. Let dry.
3 Enlarge and trace deer onto tracing paper, cut out, and trace onto brown paper; cut out brown paper.
4 Use hot glue to attach deer, greens, flowers, berries, and ribbon.
5 For the lid cut or tear a piece of decorative textured red paper and layer it with smaller cream-color torn paper squares. If desired, use a square crocheted doily or paper. Highlight the edges of the papers with a small amount of gold highlighting medium applied to your finger. Adhere all pieces on the lid using hot glue and finish with porcelain flowers, berries, and greenery.
6 Use crafts glue to apply sheer ribbon or trim around edge.

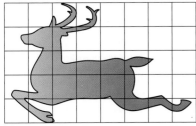

1 Square = 1 Inch

Christmas Deer Box Pattern
Enlarge at 400%

Delightfully Dotted Tapers

shown on page 141

WHAT YOU NEED

  Freezer paper
  Tea light candle
  Matches
  Metallic red or green tapers
  Gold sealing wax (normally used to
    seal envelopes)
  Old candle

HERE'S HOW

1 Cover the work surface with the freezer paper.
2 Light tea light candle with a match. Lay candle taper flat on the work surface. Light the stick of sealing wax and immediately begin dropping dots of wax onto an old candle for practice.
3 Make one row of dots down the taper and extinguish the stick of sealing wax (otherwise the burning wax stick will continue to drip wax very quickly and will use up a lot of wax). Keep the taper firmly in place while the wax dots harden. Rocking the taper to one side or another before the wax has set will result in the wax running around the side of the taper. Repeat this process to apply additional wax dots to the tapers.

Personalized Pillow

shown on page 142

WHAT YOU NEED

  Solid-color throw pillow with
    removable covering
  White monogrammed linen napkin
  Straight pins
  White thread; sewing needle
  Four ½-inch white buttons

HERE'S HOW

1 Remove the pillow from the case. Center the linen napkin on the pillowcase front and pin in place.
2 Sew buttons on each corner of the napkin, securing it to the pillowcase.
3 Reinsert the pillow in the case.

Christmas Jubilee Garland

shown on pages 142–143

WHAT YOU NEED

  Fine wire; wire cutter
  Long sewing needle
  Pinecones; seedpods; cranberries
    and apples, real or artificial
  Jingle bells; hand drill or ice pick

HERE'S HOW

1 Cut a piece of wire the desired garland length; thread needle with wire.
2 Determine a pattern for the garland. String on the items in the set pattern to fill the wire, drilling or poking holes through the items when necessary. Wrap the wire around the end items to prevent the items from slipping off.

tabletops
by the dozen

Welcome family and guests to your dinner table with glistening settings that set a joyous tone.

Whether it's a holiday party or Christmas dinner, these place settings will wow everyone at the table. The **Personalized Place Setting,** *opposite*, cleverly coordinates a picture frame coaster and a napkin ring embellished with scrapbooking letters. For extra flair, place a **Beautifully Beaded Napkin** by each plate. Instructions are on *page 156*.

In minutes you can transform a plain table into a gala gathering place. Nestle personalized glass trim in icy branches for **Wintry Wonders**, *right*. The **Holiday Music Place Setting**, *below*, comes together quickly with a themed ornament and sheet music. For a dainty **Very Vintage** arrangement, stack mismatched china, *opposite*. When time is short, choose an ornament **Made to Match** a patterned plate. Instructions are on *pages 156–157*.

The art of arranging sets the tone for celebration. Cradle a candle-lit glass punch bowl in ribbon-wrapped greens for **True Holiday Hue,** *opposite.* The playful look of **Stars All Around,** *above,* can be achieved with an easy-to-make place mat, name tag, and dish. Wrap a piece of mat board and tie it with a bow for an elegant **Present Presentation.** Instructions are on *pages 157–158.*

Make the tablescape an unforgettable field of red and green. A tea towel and crocheted hot pad are the secrets to a **Kitchen Classic** look, *right*. For a **Winter White Arrangement,** *below,* create a still life using white dishes warmed with glowing candles and sprigs of greenery. You'll want to use **Woven Ribbon Poinsettia Mats,** *opposite,* for all your dressiest holiday dinners. Instructions are on *pages 158–159.*

Personalized Place Setting

shown on page 148

WHAT YOU NEED

5×7-inch decorative picture frame
Silver art paper; scissors
Scrapbooking letters; velvet ribbon

HERE'S HOW

1 For the coaster, use a decorative 5×7-inch picture frame. Cut silver art paper to fit in the frame and place it under the glass. Assemble the frame.

2 To create a personalized place card, transform a napkin ring with purchased scrapbooking letters in each guest's initials. Attach the letters to velvet ribbon and tie it around a folded napkin. Use silver-tone flatware to coordinate with the picture frame.

Beautifully Beaded Napkins

shown on page 149

WHAT YOU NEED

Thread to match napkin color
Beading needle

Striped fabric dinner napkins
Small round glass beads in teal, blue, orange, and green
Seed beads in green, teal, blue, red, orange, and silver
Sequins in star, flower, leaf, and snowflake shapes

HERE'S HOW

1 Thread the beading needle and knot the end. Starting at the bottom right corner of the napkin, bring the thread up from the underside so the knot remains hidden. Avoid making a single stitch with more than four or five beads. Larger bead loops might sag or snag and won't lay flat against the fabric. Follow each sequin with a seed bead, then only stitch back through the sequin to anchor it to the fabric.

2 *For the tree* start at the base and work up the trunk adding branches to either side on the way back down.

3 *For the snowflake* start in the center with a snowflake sequin, add smaller sequins and beads around the edges.

4 *For the flowers* start at the base of the stems and work up to the flowers, stopping halfway to form the leaves. End by layering sequins and beads to make the flower.

Wintry Wonders

shown on page 150

WHAT YOU NEED

Metallic gold marking pen
Small clear glass square ornament
Silver snowflake stickers
Gold and silver ribbons
Iced branches

HERE'S HOW

1 Use a gold marking pen to write the guest's name on the ornament. Accent the ornament with snowflake stickers.

2 Tie ribbons onto the hanger. Arrange the ornament with iced branches alongside the place setting.

Very Vintage

shown on page 151

WHAT YOU NEED

Unmatched china (family heirlooms if possible); white linens
Coordinating gold-tone ornament
Thin gold cord or ribbon

HERE'S HOW

1 For a vintage look, layer unmatched china with largest plate at the bottom and accent it with crisp white linens.
2 Thread an ornament with gold cord or ribbon and place on the plate.

Holiday Music Place Setting

shown on page 150

WHAT YOU NEED

Photocopy of old music printed on card stock paper
Decorative-edge scissors
Stapler; napkin
Purchased instrument ornament
Desired dishes (white or black work best)
3-inch square of blue cardstock
White parchment paper
Permanent marking pens in gold and black; hole punch
12-inch-length of striped ribbon

HERE'S HOW

1 Use decorative-edge scissors to cut the printed music paper into a 1½×8-inch strip. Curve the strip around to form a napkin holder and staple together. Roll the napkin and slide it through the holder. Place the holder on the dishes.
2 Lay the ornament next to the napkin.
3 Trim the parchment to fit atop the blue card stock. Write the guest's name on the parchment using the marking pens. Punch a hole in the corner and thread the ribbon through the hole; tie to the holder and napkin.

Made to Match

shown on page 151

WHAT YOU NEED

⅛-inch coordinating ribbon in 2 colors
Holiday-design dinner plate
Small ornament in design similar to plate
Coordinating flatware
Solid cloth napkin
Charger to match napkin

HERE'S HOW

1 Tie ribbons to the ornament hanger, leaving long tails. Arrange the ornament, along with the flatware, napkin, and dinner plate on the charger.

True Holiday Hue

shown on page 152

WHAT YOU NEED

Newspapers
Clear glass punch bowl
Thick white crafts glue
Red glitter
Red votive candles
Clear glass votive candleholders
Greenery
Holly and berries
1½-inch-wide red and green ribbon

HERE'S HOW

1 Cover the work surface with newspapers. Squeeze a line of glue just below the lip of the punch bowl. While glue is wet, sprinkle with glitter and let dry.
2 Place votives in holders and arrange in the punch bowl.
3 Surround the bowl with greenery, holly, and berries.
4 Tie a generous ribbon bow to embellish the front of the arrangement.

Present Presentation

shown on page 153

WHAT YOU NEED

16-inch square mat board
Wrapping paper; tape; scissors
2⅞-inch-wide red ribbon
Gold metallic napkin
Clear glass charger; small boxes

HERE'S HOW

1 Cover the mat board with wrapping paper, taping on the back.
2 Cut two 20-inch lengths of ribbon. Cross the ribbon in the center of the square; tape the ends to the back.
3 Place the charger in mat center. Tie a 20-inch length of ribbon around the napkin and place it on the charger. Place small boxes wrapped with coordinating paper at the mat top.

Stars All Around Pattern
Enlarge at 800%

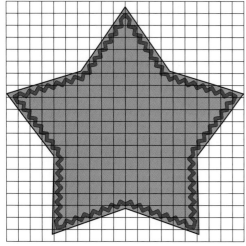

1 Square = 1 Inch

Stars All Around

shown on page 153

WHAT YOU NEED

Tracing paper; pencil; scissors
Two 24-inch squares of green sportweight fabric
Fusible webbing; iron
Batting; sewing machine; thread
2 yards of ¾-inch red chenille rickrack
1 yard of ⅜-inch green velvet ribbon
Purchased name tag
5-inch brass star shape for name tag
Pinking shears

HERE'S HOW

1 Enlarge, trace, and cut out pattern, *left*. Use pattern to cut out two star shapes from green sportweight fabric. Cut one star shape from fusible webbing. Cut one star shape from batting, trimming an extra ¾ inch from outer edge.
2 Fuse webbing to wrong side of one green fabric star according to manufacturer's instructions. Layer stars with wrong sides together and batting between. Fuse together. Pink the edge.
3 Machine-stitch rickrack ¾ inch from edge around outer edge of star.
4 For place card ornament tie the velvet ribbon bow and name tag onto the brass star.

Kitchen Classic

shown on page 154

WHAT YOU NEED

Vintage red plaid tea towels
Vintage dishes; flatware
Crocheted hot pads in red, green, and white
½-inch-wide green ribbon; scissors

HERE'S HOW

1 Use a red plaid tea towel for a napkin and set by plate.
2 Place a hot pad near the plate top for a coaster and one on the plate.
3 Tie flatware with a ribbon bow. Place cookies cutters at the plate top.

Winter White Arrangement

shown on page 154

WHAT YOU NEED

White glass punch bowl
White glass platter
Assorted white glass containers, such as creamers, bowls, and pitchers
Assorted white candles
Greenery, berries, and candy sticks
Berry wreath

Ⓐ

HERE'S HOW

1 For the base overturn a punch bowl and top with a platter. Arrange containers atop the platter.

2 Fill with candles and tuck in greenery, berries, and candy sticks. Encircle the base with a berry wreath.

Woven Ribbon Poinsettia Mat

shown on page 155

WHAT YOU NEED

Scissors; 6½ yards of 2¾-inch
   white double-faced satin ribbon
1½ yards of 2¾-inch green
   double-face satin ribbon
Masking tape; sewing machine
Thread; spray fabric adhesive
Silver metallic machine thread
Two 14×20-inch rectangles of
   white felt; fabric tacky glue
Tracing paper; pencil
Fusible webbing
5×16-inch piece each of red felt in
   two different shades
2×12-inch piece of green felt
12 red and silver jewelry findings,
   such as Crystal Innovations
18-inch square of metallic red
   fabric for napkin

HERE'S HOW

1 To make a 14×20-inch mat, cut five 24-inch-lengths of white ribbon for the horizontal pieces. Cut six 18-inch lengths of white ribbon for the vertical pieces. Cut one 18-inch length of green ribbon for a vertical band.

2 On a smooth surface arrange the horizontal white ribbons, taping ends to secure as necessary. Start weaving 2 inches in from edge, working left to right with the second row using green ribbon. Continue weaving with white vertical ribbons.

3 Use spray adhesive to attach one white felt piece to weaving. Carefully remove tape and machine-quilt with silver thread diagonally across the ribbon squares through all layers as shown in Photo A, *right*. Use fabric glue to secure ribbon ends to wrong side. Glue on a felt backing piece.

4 Enlarge and trace six poinsettia shapes, *right*, onto fusible webbing. According to manufacturer's instructions, fuse and cut out three red felt shapes, each of the two shades. Work in same manner for the green felt holly leaves.

5 Layer the dark red felt over the lighter shade. Arrange poinsettias and leaves onto place mat. With minimal fusing secure poinsettias and leaves to place mat. With silver machine thread and a zigzag stitch, detail the centers of poinsettias and leaves, securing to the place mat.

6 Sew three jewelry findings to center of poinsettia as shown in Photo B.

7 *For red napkin* stitch with silver top thread over two-ply using a zigzag stitch ½ inch from the outer edge. Fringe the edge as desired.

8 *For napkin ring* make a poinsettia as in Steps 4 and 5, *above*; stitch to the center of a yard of green ribbon. Tie it around the napkin.

Ⓑ

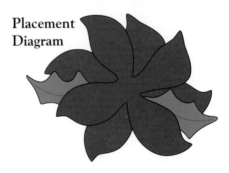

Placement Diagram

Woven Ribbon Poinsettia
Enlarge at 200%

1 Square = 1 Inch

index

sources

BOTTLE CAPS
Li'l Davis Designs
www.lildavisdesigns.com

CIGAR BOX PURSES
Plaid Enterprises, Inc.
Norcross, GA 30091-7600
800-842-4197
www.plaidonline.com

CLAY TEXTURE SHEETS
Polyform Products
1901 Estes Avenue
Elk Grove, IL 60007
www.sculpey.com

EMBOSSING METAL
American Art Clay Co., Inc.
4717 W. 16th Street
Indianapolis, IN 46222

FINISHES, PAINTS, STENCILS
Delta Technical Coatings, Inc.
2550 Pellissier Place
Whittier, CA 90601
www.deltacrafts.com

MINIATURE MARBLES
Halcraft USA, Inc.
30 West 24th Street
New York, NY 10010
212-376-1580

MOSAIC GROUT AND TILES
Clearly Mosaics—The Beadery Craft Products
P.O. Box 178
Hope Valley, RI, 02832
401-539-2432
www.thebeadery.com

PIGMENT INK PADS
Clearsnap Inc.
Box 98
Anacortes, WA 98221
800-448-4862
www.clearsnap.com

RIBBON
Midori, Inc.
708 6th Avenue North
Seattle, WA 98109
800-659-3049
www.midoriribbon.com

STONE PAINT
Krylon Products Group
Cleveland, OH 44115
800-4-KRYLON (457-9566)
www.krylon.com